STUCK

Break Through the Deception Hidden in Reality

and Find Your Way Back Home

Wilkes-Barre

Wilkes-Barre
www.ARISBooks.com

Awakening: Break Through the Deception Hidden in Reality and Find Your Way Back Home. Copyright © 2024 by Stefan Becker. All rights reserved. No part of this book may be reproduced or transmitted in any form or by any means, electronic or mechanical, including photocopying, recording, or by any information storage and retrieval system, without permission in writing from the publisher, except by a reviewer, who may quote brief passages in review.

ARIS Books' titles may be bulk purchased for business or promotional use or for special sales. Please contact ARIS Books for more information.

ARIS Books is an imprint of and its name and logo are trademarks of Kallisti Publishing Inc. All rights reserved.

Please note that any errors, typographical or otherwise, are here for a purpose: some people actually enjoy looking for them and we strive to please as many people as possible. If you would like to report a typo or error, please contact us via our web site — *https://arisbooks.com/report-a-typo*.

ISBN-13 978-1-7359792-9-8

Library of Congress Control Number: 2024910641

DESIGNED & PRINTED IN THE UNITED STATES OF AMERICA

CONTENTS

PREFACE FOR THE ENGLISH LANGUAGE EDITION
I

PREFACE
III

PART 1
HOW IT ALL BEGAN AND WHAT CAME AFTERWARDS
1

PART 2
DEVELOPING AWARENESS
95

PART 3
OUR AWAKENING
159

EPILOGUE
183

GRID WORLD

I am on the run.

In the process, I run through a world consisting entirely of grids.

Grid corridors and grid stairs leading up, down, right, and left.

I am being followed and I am aware that all the other people have already been captured and are locked behind the barred doors that line the corridors through which I run.

I am aware that they are closing in on me and that I must hurry on my flight.

I now reach another barred door.

Here I stop and turn into a bird.

I immediately fly through the keyhole of the barred door in front of me, which thus opens.

The people having been imprisoned behind that door now regain liberty.

PREFACE FOR THE ENGLISH LANGUAGE EDITION

About a year ago, on August 29, 2022, I have self-published my book *Erwachen* in German language. Shortly afterwards, the idea arose to also publish an English language version which now has finally been finished. It took my wife and me about 4 months to complete the translation and to get this version ready to publish.

I have spent part of my life residing in Canada and the US. What became obvious to me is, that in North America people are much more open and willing to allow for controversial topics and thoughts to be discussed. In Germany, the mainstream agenda is deeply ingrained into the thought processes of the vast majority of the populace, and thus it is difficult to find an audience of open-minded people for any approach to the general idea of reality that diverts from the traditional ways of understanding.

In *Awakening*, I want to invite you on a journey, beginning in Part 1 with my own life's path and then leading in Part 2 to the insights that I have gained along the way. Insights regarding what is happening on earth, who we are, where we have come from, where we are meant to go, and how most urgent it has become that we step into our true self and awaken to it.

Looking at how government, science, education, and media are nowadays jointly pushing one artificially implemented worldwide narrative after another upon humanity, it becomes ever more urgent to free oneself from these all-encompassing clutches. First, we need to take a close look at what is happening and how, which will give us an understanding about where this is supposed to lead and what humanity's role in this is supposed to be. My impression is that for the most part, we have not yet faced reality head-on. And because of that, we look for solutions within a system that has been built so that no solution can be found within it that can free ourselves from it. So, at best we are running in circles or move to more remote areas of our prison. Once we have faced reality as it is, we can embark on a path which will lead us to where we were meant to go when

AWAKENING

entering this incarnation on earth.

This is what I envision with this book. That we join forces together and make our awakening happen. For us, for all of humanity, and for all living beings on earth. That we reconnect with the All-One. The All-Oneness from were we all once embarked on our journey through life. Part 3 of this book will be providing suggestions and ideas as to how we can accomplish this together.

So, let's get going and hopefully we will meet soon to bring this book to life in a practical way.

Encarnacion, Paraguay
July 1, 2023

PREFACE

Time and again I intended to write a book. About my life, my encounters, my thoughts, my dreams, and my journeys. And then I put it off and put it off again.

The world is currently changing rapidly, and it seems more and more urgent to me that we wake up and understand what is going on around us. What is going on and what has been going on for so much longer than we can imagine.

The time to awaken is NOW. Actually, it was yesterday.

To be able to awaken, we must realize where we are and above all, who we are, beyond abstractive concepts. It is also not necessary that we all awaken at the same time. It is only necessary that those who have voluntarily incarnated into this epoch as light workers, pathfinders, or star children remember their mission, for which they have prepared long and thoroughly. They open the doors to the divine Light and knowledge. For earthbound humanity. The global agenda in all its excesses is dedicated to prevent this on all levels, including through alternative channels and "spiritual teachers." More on this later.

Grid World is the title of my dream from the first half of 1995, which I told at the beginning of this book. At that time, I hardly ever had been able to recall my dreams but this dream burned itself into my memory immediately, I remembered it vividly after awakening. I did not understand its message then, but I instinctively knew its importance, its urgency.

Today, 27 years later, on May 27, 2022 I see in my dream my life's mission.

How that came about and what I have encountered during the past 58 years, I will report on the following pages.

After a year of traveling and searching, from one accommodation to the next, I arrived yesterday in the south of Paraguay, in the city of Encarnacion. Right now, I am living on a main thoroughfare in a small room, and life is clearly telling me that I must start this book, because otherwise it will be too late.

I will let my intuition guide me in writing the following chapters. I do not have a concept, just an essence that I want to convey.

Thank you for getting this book. We are all facing the most

exciting moments of all time, and it is important that we do not miss this great event. If we open to the world of our origin, our true being now, then we will be right up front and take as many people as possible with us on this journey.

Here we go.

__Encarnacion, Paraguay__
__May 27, 2022__

PART 1

HOW IT ALL BEGAN AND WHAT CAME AFTERWARDS

1964 to 1969 : Hamburg and USA

After my birth in Hamburg in May 1964, my mother left me quite soon and married another man. I came to live with my grandparents, where the relationship between them was strained. Two years later my mother returned to my father and me, but this separation of my parents caused me injuries that influence me and my life until today. My brother was born in 1967, and in the same year we moved to the United States, where we lived for the next two years, in Texas and in Arizona. There my father trained as a fighter pilot for the German Air Force.

During the years in the USA, I threw myself into a large pool several times, and I still remember vividly how I sank to the ground without any fear, looking upwards. Today, I suspect that at that time I wanted to return to my soul's homeland. This earth was not my home and I did not belong in the world of humans either.

I am sitting here writing these lines over fifty years later, which means that I have been rescued from the pool again and again. After each rescue my soul cried out its frustration about it. Of course, it did not help and nobody understood me. My rescuer was repeatedly a very young woman from Germany who had followed her slightly older husband to his pilot training in the USA. I can still see her swimming underwater towards me.

1969 to 1978 : North Frisia

In 1969 my family went back to Germany, to North Frisia, where I spent my childhood until 1978. I struggled at school and just about managed to get through secondary school. I was constantly reading and spending time alone in nature, growing trees and flowers from seeds and offshoots, sitting for hours at a hidden pond and looking at life under the surface of the water. At school I was the whipping boy and at home I felt misunderstood and was criticized for my peculiarity to an ever-increasing degree by my father. Life "out there" began to fill me with more and more fear and anxiety as the years went by. Especially the life grown ups were leading in society.

During the years in North Frisia, I began to have slight

supra-sensory perceptions, especially in the evenings before I went to sleep. For example, the space above me became endlessly wide and I found myself in these moments in a state free of the fears and limitations of the human world. During this time, almost every night before going to sleep, my imagination carried me alone in a spaceship into the vastness of space. I was there in search of new living spaces, and this search took unimaginable periods of time.

Childhood Dreams

As a child, I had two constant dreams again and again over many years.

In the first dream I was alone in a small space capsule with which I orbited the earth. This capsule entered the earth's atmosphere again and again after a certain time, and during this process I regularly suffocated in the capsule.

In my second dream I found myself in a crashed flying object, in which there were no further survivors. Then a giant came and rescued me, by putting me on his shoulders, from the scene of the accident.

Today, I see in these dreams a description of my experiences at the beginning of my incarnation into this life. It was difficult and, to put it mildly, fraught with problems. I learned more about this during a regression a month ago which I will report about in a later chapter.

My childhood and adolescence were characterized by an increasing fear of society and the world around me. I felt like an outsider in almost all aspects here and could not imagine any role of my own in life and the community at all.

On the one hand, I was already aware at the age of 12 that one can manifest things and de-manifest them again at will and as needed, through mentally influencing antimatter and matter. On the other hand, at the beginning of my secondary education I had the deep conviction that it makes no sense at all to enter a working life where one goes to work every day for decades and repeats the same tasks over and over again. I was firmly convinced that if you did the work once, that was enough.

Later, these ideas seemed phantasmagorical to me, and more and more I gave in to the "reality" of daily life.

Books

During my time in North Frisia, I encountered two stories that would later, and especially in the present time, be of importance for my understanding of what is happening in our world.

First, this was the story of John Christopher about the "tripod monsters." Therein, Christopher reports about the earth in the future. In the story, people live without technology and do all the work manually. An extraterrestrial race has discovered the earth as an alternative place to their home planet, on which the environment did no longer allow these beings to survive. These extraterrestrials can exist on the earth at first only in habitats with artificially maintained climatic conditions. The earth must be changed atmospherically and biospherically, in order to make possible for these beings a life outside of their protected biospheres. So that this could be done without resistance of the earth inhabitants, mankind was brought by means of technical aids under a mental control which ensured that on the one hand nobody rebels or understands this plan, and on the other hand mankind can be used without causing problems as manpower for the necessary preparation of the earth's conversion and for the current supply of the extraterrestrials in their dwellings.

The control of the people is achieved by the extraterrestrials by implanting a metal grid into people's scalps upon completion of the 14th year of their life, which serves as a receiver for the signals with which the thoughts and emotions of humans are controlled and manipulated.

Today, other authors such as Dean Koontz in the *Jane Hawk* series, describe how the injection of nano-particles by means of two syringes given at certain time intervals causes neuronal networks to form in the brain from the self-assembling nanoparticles. It is also interesting to note that these syringes must remain chilled to -70 degrees before administration. Via these nano-networks, the affected people can then be completely remote-controlled.

The second book has the title *Der Spiegelplanet* (*The Mirror Planet*) by Mark Brandis (pseudonym). Mark Brandis and his crew have been taken far off course by a pulsar and are trying to find a course back to Earth, which proves to be difficult. Completely by surprise, a planet appears which looks like the earth. Only it is not supposed to be found in this area. They fly to the planet and send an excursion team onto its surface.

Very quickly it becomes obvious that this is a mirror planet of the Earth, which looks the same on the outside but is inhabited by a very differently developed culture and society. It has just been decided on the part of the government of this planet that it is dangerous for humans to live freely on the land or in small communities. In order to protect humanity, all citizens must move to large cities built specifically for this purpose, by a deadline that is fast approaching. After the deadline, people who are still outside the cities will be shot by security forces.

The cities are hermetically enclosed in border fortifications and no one is allowed to leave them. The people are not supposed to work anymore either, they can order everything they need via devices installed in every apartment, and this is delivered automatically and computerized via the device into the apartment. Goods and foodstuffs are produced by means of completely automated processes.

I read these books in the second half of the 70s, and the parallels to today's social development are frightening. You'll see more in the second part of this book.

1978 to 1988 : Breisgau, the Rhineland, and the first step into adult life

After the years in North Frisia, my family moved to Freiburg/Breisgau, and I felt like a badly transplanted tree. In the little over 2½ years in Freiburg, I was able towards the end to settle in, albeit with difficulty. More and more I got involved with photography and depicted the world as I saw it in photos. Even though school did not give me any pleasure and I had hardly any interest of my own in any subject, it became more and more a purpose for me to postpone the start of a job or an apprenticeship into the future. Also, by achieving good grades, I began to create a certain *raison d'être* for myself in my own mind, for my parents, and for society. I was able to continue this for two more years when my family had to move again, this time to the Rhineland. There I made the specialized high school diploma in economics. After moving away from Freiburg, however, I was never again really at home anywhere.

The seriousness of life hit me with full force when I had to remain alone in the Rhineland after graduating from school at the age of 19 to complete my training as an industrial business man. My family moved once again to North Frisia, and from there I took the train back to the Rhineland alone at the end of the summer vacations to start my training there, living in my own room.

After just a few days, I went to my training manager and handed in my notice. I had gotten myself a rental car (due to my age, I was only given a VW Beetle) and wanted to drive back to my family with it and all my belongings that I could fit in it. Acquaintances who heard of my plan told my parents about it, and, shocked, they visited me the next weekend and dissuaded me from my plan. It was agreed that I could come home for a long weekend every 3 weeks, and so I got through the 1¾ years of training. Here, too, I managed to graduate quite successful.

Thus, to the outside world, my neat grades gave the impression that I fit into society to a certain extent. Inside, however, things looked quite different. After my 15-month military service, I took up a position as a controller in the company where I had been trained. I was lucky enough to meet a boss there who became my mentor, who taught me a lot and respected me in all my limitations. During this time, my parents moved back to the Rhineland and I was able to live at home again. However, since it was clear that the moment when I would have to leave my parents' house permanently was getting closer and closer, I began to feel anxious, which expressed itself for two years in a row in several deep depressions that lasted for months. I hardly ate anything, and outside of my work I lived completely withdrawn in my room. My parents apparently did not notice my condition.

I had no self-esteem worth mentioning beyond my good grades, and I could not imagine being able to exist in the world outside the parental home.

PART 1

1988 to 1995 : Anxieties, the grid dream, and new beginnings

In order to avoid the threat of being forced to move out of my parents' house (at the latest, a new professional transfer of my father would have led to this), I registered with a dating agency in order to meet a girlfriend. In my normal life there was nothing like that and I was already 24-years-old. With a lot of effort and after many attempts, I found a girlfriend with whom I finally moved into a shared apartment after a complicated and awkward start.

Unfortunately, only a formal partnership developed which was mainly due to my inability to relate and my psychological injuries from childhood. After four years, my girlfriend left me and this plunged me into an existential crisis. I ate almost nothing, lost weight down to the bones, and locked myself in my office for hours to cry. There are no suitable words of gratitude for the fact that my boss helped me through all this. Good friends have accompanied me out of this deep well of depression, and I regained my strength over time.

I am telling all this because I think it becomes clear here how incompatible I am with the world as we know it. This includes the fact that I have not been able to cope with computer applications and other modern communication technology from the very beginning. My real mission lies elsewhere, as it does with a whole range of people to whom this book is urgently addressed.

It should be mentioned that in the years between 1983 and 2000, I had such dramatic nightmares that I sometimes jumped out of bed in my sleep, woke up the whole house screaming, and once I even stood up against the wall and shouted for help, because in my sleeping perception there were intruders in my room. Several times in my sleep I had the feeling that a huge celestial body was crashing down on me from above, and in my sleep, I tried to physically avoid it.

In 1995 I attended an adult education course in autogenic training. This was my first contact with a spiritual subject and spiritual practice. During this time, my grid dream appeared and I met my soul mate.

That was the beginning of a parallel life, which has brought me into touch with many spiritual topics, trainings, journeys, teachers, and studies over 27 years. This entire time was characterized by the fact that I gained more and more insights, and in the first 10 years many dreams flooded my sleep every night. However, I had no extrasensory perceptions of my own and no conscious contact with ethereal or supernatural beings of any kind.

1995 until today : from where to where

The following is the story of my path from 1995 until today. I am writing down these recollections from memory and would like to show the influences and inspirations which have contributed to the conclusions and insights which I will present in the further course of this book. Time and again I have been led to certain information and situations that I would not have been able to find myself and that have always built on each other, always expanding my horizon of knowledge. I walked this path together with my soul mate. When she moved into my apartment in October 1995, she brought with her, among other things, a book whose title already contained a reference to our common mission. *Woher Wohin (From Where to Where)* was the title of the book by Walther Hinz, which for me was the beginning of a study of spiritual and esoteric writings and teachings which continues to this day.

Our first stop was a partnership/perception seminar with Günter Sellin in the Saarland in September 1995. There, a painful confrontation with my inner blockages, fears, and limitations began. Mostly I felt threatened in such situations, because I regularly expected that my inadequacy would be recognized and thus it would also become obvious to my soul mate that she must leave me. This was one of my greatest fears at that time.

Subsequently, in the spring of 1996, we began to attend dream workshops and dream groups, and consciously dealt with the language of dreams and the understanding of our dreams. In 1997, I started a 2-year training program in analytical dreamwork with Helmut Hark, Hanna Laross, and Maria Schunk-Warning. I was the only participant there who was not a therapist and I was also the youngest in the group. During this time, I studied extensively the work of C.G. Jung and his students. Topics like symbolism and numerology, but also astrology from a Jungian point of view were part of it. In the years 1997 to 1999, I intensively studied the work of Slovenian geomancer Marko Pogacnik, including my participation in three earth healing events. There Marko spoke about the fact that we are facing a very special, unprecedented moment in the history of the universe. Not only the world of human beings, but also the world of spiritual entities and the entire remainder of the universe would evolve to a higher level of vibration. Through Marko and the Geomancy School Hagia Chora, which organized these events, I learned a lot about the topics of subtle perception, elemental beings, landscape temples, and geomancy. I discovered Nikola Tesla, Rudolf Steiner, Zecheria Sitchin, Christa Zettel, and many other spiritual authors and teachers during this time. I also attended workshops with Peter Dawkins on Zoence, a western form of Feng Shui, and with Art Reade, a shaman from Arizona. We participated in family constellations and met weekly in a small group with a Reiki Master, where we were accompanied on guided meditative journeys. During this time, it became more and more clear to me that something in this world is not right or needs transformation.

The third party in the group : Canada

In 1996, a holiday trip led us to a lonely property in the middle of the forest at Powell Lake in British Columbia, Canada. This site was only accessible by a 2-hour boat ride, there was no electricity, of course no Internet yet, only a radio station from Nanaimo that we were able to receive. We spent 3 weeks there in the wild lush nature, and these weeks left such a deep impression on us that we started to investigate the possibilities of emigrating to North America. A good friend from our meditation group happened to move to Vancouver, BC, in 1997, and after we decided in early 1998 to emigrate to BC, too, we prepared our application for a residence permit together with her. During a one-week visit in February 1998, we accompanied her to a service at the Unity Church in Burnaby (not to be confused with the United Church). Unity Church, and especially the minister at the time, Marvin Anderson, provided a broad approach to general and alternative spirituality and wisdom in the Sunday service. In particular, he mentioned at that time that the 6 weeks before Easter are a highly potent time in which to put one's desires and intentions into action, in which one has a heavenly tailwind, so to speak, for this. So, we decided to finish our application for permanent residency in Canada during the weeks until Easter, which was a herculean task as it turned out afterwards. As a support, our friend sent us a tape recording of each current church service with Marvin by mail every week. Since immigration was much easier for married couples (only one partner needed to fulfill the necessary requirements), we spontaneously went to the registry office and asked for the next possible date for a wedding. On April 3, 1998, the wedding date arrived, one week before Good Friday.

And at this point began a miraculous passage of time, which brought us to Canada in record time. According to the Canadian embassy, the processing of the documents would take between 12- and 18-months, combined with an interview in the embassy. We received after only two months the request for a medical examination, and two months later, on August 11, 1998, we received our documents for the immigration which were valid for ten months. We quit our jobs and set the date for the emigration to the last day of my training in dream analysis, the 2nd of May, 1999.

As soon as we landed in Vancouver, BC, my insecurities and fears caught up with me mightily. I panicked and wanted to return to Germany as soon as possible. Our friend and my wife convinced me to stay. From one contact to another and one "coincidence" to the next, we were then led to Nelson, BC and on to a house in Kaslo, BC. We had come to love Kaslo in the summer of 1998 on a tour of southern British Columbia, and we imagined with great naivety that our Canadian home could be there.

At that time, it was still common practice to look for rental houses through newspaper ads and phone calls. We asked at a pizzeria in the small town of Kaslo for a public phone booth. When asked what had brought us to Kaslo, we talked about our house hunt. The owner of the pizzeria happened to know a house owner who had just come back from Australia to live in his house for a week and would then travel on to Toronto with his family. He called him and sent us to this house. It was located four miles outside the small village of Kaslo with its 1,000 inhabitants, and was situated on a huge property above Kootenay Lake. The landlord immediately perceived us as suitable tenants, especially since we would be able to pay a year's rent in advance and made a reliable impression. The house had a large living/dining area, three baths, three bedrooms, a hobby room, a TV room, large decks, a huge garage, a basement with exercise equipment, and a pool table. I was overwhelmed by this place and at first, I did not want to decide for it.

However, a dream and a special incident made us go there once more.

First, I had a dream in which I was told that if I did not complete the last year of high school, I would never be able to study. To me, that was a clear message at that time: "If you don't stay here, it will have a very negative impact on your path." Nevertheless, we initially inspected more houses, with one appointment being more depressive than the next.

After we had done our last house hunting, we sat in our car and I literally sank down into a deep mental gloom and apathy. Deeper and deeper, I lost myself, and then suddenly out of the blue, all the vents in our car came on at full blast; my consciousness was literally jerked back from the depths of darkness. After I got the ventilation back under control by starting the engine, we decided to drive again to the big house from our first visit, to sense if we could imagine living there. The landlord saw us from a distance and then did his best to convince us to rent from him. And thus began an intense time that would never have been imaginable to me in advance . . .

Our house in Kaslo came fully furnished including all other equipment, with books, CDs, videos, pictures, flowers, chickens, and plenty of fruit trees as well as a canoe. The book collection also included some spiritual works, among others a book by Solara with the title *11:11*. For the second time now, I encountered the concept that very soon a big advancement of our consciousness should take place. According to Solara, the current evolutionary cycle entered its final phase in 1987 at the Harmonic Convergence, and for this event Solara began a 24-year long quest with a powerful ritual at the Cheops Pyramid, a journey which would lead her to many spiritually relevant places on Earth up until the year 2011. In the process, the energy portals representing those places were activated. In the book *11:11*, Solara spoke about the fact that until 2011, a higher vibrating level of consciousness would partially overlap with the previous level of consciousness, *i.e.*, the one in which the earth currently is. During this time of superimposition, the opportunity opens to change from our present world of experience into a higher vibrational one. This book fascinated me very much and resonated deeply with me.

In the book collection, we also found some works by Omraam Mikhael Aivanhov, of whom we had not heard before. Aivanhov hailed from Bulgaria and followed his compatriot and teacher Peter Deunov. Aivanhov's writings cover subjects such as eurythmy, movement, music and vibration, astrology, art, nutrition, and many other matters. At that time, our landlords had mentioned that there was a community of followers of these two spiritual teachers from Bulgaria in a place called Jaffray, about 90 miles away. Some time later, we decided to drive to Jaffray, BC on the off-chance to find this community. Although the town is quite small, we found no sign of this group there. Finally, we asked at the local post office, where they looked at us cluelessly. However, they did know of a place called "Ideal Guest Ranch," although they did not know what occupations the people there were engaged in.

The ranch was quite remote and the people there looked at us very surprised when we drove up. We told them about our search, and our interlocutors then disappeared into a house. After some time, a lady came out, Soer Natasha, who was indeed the leader of the community in the spirit of Mikhael Aivanhov. She remarked that it was quite unusual for guests to appear there out of the blue; they lived very secretively and in fact no one knew who they were. But since we had appeared there, there was surely a deeper meaning behind it. We were invited to participate in the spiritual and worldly life of the community for 2 days and were given a room for the night.

PART 1

Within a few hours, we were lovingly and patiently introduced by members of this group to the basic ideas of Aivanhov's teachings and the way of life of the community. We listened to the special chants that go back to Aivanhov and Deunov, as well as to various lectures.

According to my understanding, such encounters bring about something in the depths of our being. Vibrations, e.g., through music, enter our cells and flow through our soul. There they create resonances, awaken memories, or transfer knowledge.

Contrary to the stories and narratives of many esoteric and spiritual teachers, I have not experienced any conscious awakening experiences or flashes of inspiration during encounters like the one in Jaffray. I have also at no time consciously had contact with beings from other dimensions or other levels of being, nor have I been given any spiritual transmissions that I could write down. However, I notice that despite this lack of communication with the spiritual worlds, I am continuously led to certain places, certain people, special books, and the like. Much of the information and ideas I encounter build on each other and bring me to my own realizations about the meaning of our being and the path we are walking. The corresponding concepts simply arise in me, they do not originate from any deliberation. Very often, I simply tell my wife about thoughts that are going through my mind, and then narratives unfold as I speak, without me knowing the contents beforehand or having thought them through. Unfortunately, I can only vaguely remember many thoughts later, which also makes writing this book difficult for me. To help with this, I have asked my inner guidance to support me since it has prompted me to do this book project, so that the essence of what I want to convey and share can flow into these lines.

During the months in Kaslo, we were of course increasingly preoccupied with the question of what our future there should look like. With only a moderate knowledge of English and professional experience limited to office work, the prospects of ever being able to earn a living there looked very poor.

The fourth party in the group : the Ashram

We got the idea of opening a bookstore. At a tarot reading in Nelson, I brought up the subject and was told about a special bookstore that was supposed to be on the other side of Kootenay Lake in an ashram. There are two different ferry routes across this lake, and the first one did not get us anywhere. The second ferry took us to Kootenay Bay, from where signs led to Yasodhara Ashram. This ashram is located by the lake in the middle of the forest, at that time only accessible by a long gravel road.

We parked in front of the first building and looked around curiously. When I saw a man dressed completely in white coming out of the building, the whole thing looked scary to me; I imagined an ashram community to be some kind of sect, and this man confirmed my prejudices. I started the car engine, and with great relief I drove away from the ashram. For a few weeks the idea of a bookstore and the ashram receded into the background, but came up again on October 31, 1999. This was one of the very few days during October without rain. Slowly we had gotten cabin fever, and so we made another attempt to visit the bookstore in the ashram.

This time, I was more courageous and we went directly into the entry building where the bookstore was located. We were told that it was lunchtime and that we should come back in an hour. We were welcome to explore the grounds of the ashram during lunch hour. We accepted the offer and walked in the warm autumn sun through the gardens and past the residential buildings of the ashram until we found the Temple of Divine Light. Reverently and on socks we entered the sun-drenched temple, whose round walls consisted in the lower part entirely of glass windows and glass doors. From there we could see the magnificent nature with mountains, forests, and the large lake.

Right from the beginning, in this place I felt touched in the depths of my soul. Some books by the founder of the ashram, Swami Sivananda Radha, were on display and I began to read a book called *Time to Be Holy*. What I read in it in terms of heart wisdom touched me so intensely that I immediately felt a deep longing to spend more time in this place. Inspired, we returned to the bookstore after an hour and found out about the courses offered by the ashram.

Back home, we were ready to sign up for the 3-month Yoga Development Course (YDC), which would take place from January to April of the upcoming year. We called the ashram to register, even though we had not even had a theoretical contact with yoga before. They responded to our request accordingly and asked us to first attend a shorter course to get an idea of the way of living and studying there. Somewhat disappointed, we signed up for a 5-day program in late November. In the village of Kaslo, weekly yoga classes were offered, and we took this opportunity to get a first impression of yoga. The leader of the yoga classes was already 84-years-old, and my encounters with her made a deep impression on me. Fifty years younger than her, I felt old and inflexible when she started the class. All the stretches and movements were difficult and often painful for me. It was then that I realized how quickly and extensively our body loses its ability to move and stretch when we live unilaterally and exercise unilaterally.

In November, full of joyful expectation, we started our 5-day program — "5 Days of Hidden Language" (of Hatha Yoga) — five days about the hidden language of yoga asanas. Outside, winter was slowly setting in and I was looking forward to five days of yoga in warm classrooms. What I did not know then was that Yasodhara Ashram is a Karma Yoga Ashram. And karma yoga does not take place in warm heated rooms and a cultivated atmosphere. Karma Yoga there means that together with the permanent residents of the ashram, the participants of the courses are involved in any activities necessary for the operation and maintenance of the ashram. In our case, and to my dismay, this meant that our first session took us out into the cold onto the back of a pickup truck and into a quarry. There, we had to throw boulders onto the truck bed which were needed for a slope stabilization on a road. We were busy with this for several hours and my mood darkened more and more. I paid good money for a yoga course here and ended up in a quarry right at the start in freezing cold conditions, where I had to do heavy physical work. Unbelievable. And exactly these sensations were the point of the lessons. Because, what I was also not aware of, after such an action the personal experiences and impressions had to be put down on paper with a carbon copy for the teacher, and subsequently read out in public in the group of the participants. With a lot of kind understanding, our teachers listened to the impressions of the group. Time and again there were complaints by the participants, reproaches to others, and the like. And time and again the question was returned: "What does your reaction to the circumstances have to do with you?" After only a few hours, great doubts arose in me regarding our desire for a 3-month stay under these conditions. And I understood why they did not let us register for the big 3-month course right away. In addition, the participants came from different regions of North America and I did not understand their American dialects. This affected about 70% of what was communicated. In this course, I also learned that yoga is by no means only the physical exercise, *i.e.*, Hatha Yoga, but that there are Kundalini Yoga, Mantra Yoga, Dream Yoga, Pranayama, sacred dances, and various other types of yoga that are part of each course.

For my body the five days were good, my mind however put up resistance.

At that time, I saw only the alternative of returning to Germany after just half a year in Canada, and this did not seem suitable to us, so we made ourselves sign up for the three-month YDC 2000, which was to begin in early January 2000.

Our life in November 1999 almost completely took place inside our house, which was gradually cleared out by our landlords over time because they needed their furniture and other objects now elsewhere. While it rained continuously outside and the dirt roads and streets were hardly passable anymore, we had only our beds and a camping table with camping chairs available as furniture. These circumstances motivated us to take a trip to Florida before our time in the ashram began, which took us first to Seattle, WA after an 18-hour bus ride. At that time, I was only cursorily following the events in the world; we did not have computers, Internet or television and there was only one radio station that hardly brought any news. Therefore, we were not aware that we would be there for the second day of the major demonstration against the World

Trade Organization meeting in Seattle. On the surface, however, we did not notice anything of the agitated energies in the city. After a day in Seattle, we flew to Tampa, FL via Phoenix, AZ the following day. We had booked a hotel in Tampa for one night only. With a road map purchased locally, we headed south the next day to the municipalities of Venice and Englewood. These were the southernmost towns shown on our map. We followed signs to Manasota Key and ended up at a hidden little motel right on the beach. There we waited for a few hours until the owner showed up, who was returning from abroad that day and had been delayed at the immigration office at the airport. After his arrival, we got a room there and spent a wonderful week at the Gulf of Mexico.

In retrospect and during a second visit to the same hotel in 2015, I realized how guided our journeys had been all along. We are often led to people, places, countries, books, teachers, and most of the time we are not even aware of why we are being led there. With respect to Florida and the Gulf of Mexico, there seems to be a special energy inherent in these waters. Especially during our later one-week stay in 2015, we were strengthened physically and mentally within these few days in a way that even a 6-week spa stay could not have done better. Thus, I believe that we were supposed to stay in this energetic environment in the time before the YDC 2000, in order to be up to the challenges of the course.

We finally moved to Yasodhara Ashram on December 29, 1999. The course did not start until the fifth of January 2000, which gave us time to settle into life at the ashram and specially to welcome the new millennium with the community there in a unique spirit.

The following course period was characterized by an intensive isolation of the participants from the outside world. This was of course also because at that time, nobody was equipped with a laptop or a cell phone. There were only two coin-operated payphones, one of them out in the open, and an old computer in the small ashram library, which required 20 minutes to boot up. Since our daily classes ran from 7 am to 9 pm, Monday through Saturday, and from 9 am to 9 pm on Sundays, there was hardly any opportunity for us 28 course participants to use this computer. Furthermore, there was no television and no newspaper, and during the time of the course, we participants did not leave the ashram premises. During the first few weeks I tried to keep our car free of snow so that I might escape, if necessary, but the amount of snow that fell took away this option. I would have needed snow chains and we did not even have winter tires.

Every morning at 7 am we started the day with 1¾ hours of Hatha Yoga, often with personal reflections and symbol work. After breakfast, the classes began which were always a surprise, because there was no official course schedule. And there was Karma Yoga. Tasks were not assigned according to one's wishes or abilities, but rather according to the question of where one is confronted with oneself the most and which is the greatest psychological challenge. And through this constant confrontation with the emotions caused by the work and the group, it was possible to understand oneself and one's own behavior patterns and to recognize and heal old injuries. In most cases, the teachers only asked questions, always in the presence of the group. The conclusions and solutions came from the participants themselves.

By the way, this also applied to the confrontation with one's own religiousness. Swami Radha (she had passed away already five years before our YDC) had always attached special importance to the fact that members of all religions find a place in the ashram, including atheists.

During the YDC, we were trained in techniques such as Mindwatch (which involves consciously observing one's thoughts for an hour and then writing them down, but also becoming still in the mind), and we learned sacred dances and mantras. We were guided in dream work, read the Bhagavad Gita and the Mahabharata. As part of Kundalini Yoga, we were taught knowledge about the seven chakras and how to deal with them. Breathing exercises and the teachings of Swami Sivananda were also topics. At the end of the YDC, each of us led the evening Satsang once, and we were able to play the harmonium which we had practiced in groups before. The diversity and intensity of this experience can hardly be described in words. All of us went through an often painful and demanding process of transformation and growth, and one could see it in our faces at the end of the three months. For me, the YDC was followed by a 12-day training program to become a Hatha Yoga teacher.

In the ashram, only organic food was offered, and there was no opportunity to buy conventional snacks or sweets. Life took place in the absence of radiation exposure from wi-fi, cell phone networks, or smart meters. Such an experience would be unthinkable today over such a long time.

When we drove back to the nearby town of Nelson for the first time after 3½ months, I became strongly aware of the effect my time at the ashram had had on me. I felt hopelessly overwhelmed by the noise, the hustle and bustle, and the chaos that I encountered. And at the same time Nelson is actually a lovely, cozy little town of 10,000 people.

Even before attending the YDC, I found it difficult to keep up with the demands of my job and society. After the YDC, these difficulties intensified significantly and the following years turned out to be challenging.

Our plan after leaving the ashram was to take a 12-day tour of Nova Scotia on the east coast of Canada and then to travel to North Frisia. We did this, but returned to British Columbia after only two weeks in Germany. We felt nowhere in the right place, but Canada was meanwhile closer to our hearts. My wife moved into a hastily found small apartment in Nelson, and I went back to the ashram for two months of further studies and Karma Yoga. There I worked in various projects, taught yoga, and finished my study project, which was a prerequisite for becoming a yoga teacher outside the ashram. During this time and the following month, I worked my way through 30 books and cassette tapes and wrote elaborations on the contents. My self-chosen main topic was dream interpretation. However, I mainly read and listened to standard works by Swami Sivananda and Swami Radha. As a special assignment, I was asked to work through the story about the Tibetan yogi Milarepa. Among other things, Milarepa was repeatedly instructed by his teacher to build up something, which he then had to take down again. He struggled with this very much, and this theme should also run through my life in the following two decades. My teacher probably foresaw that.

In the meantime, it had become summer and the experience of life in the ashram was easier for me during this time than during the previous course. In addition, I had one day off per week to go to Nelson to visit my wife. These months were very pleasant for us, yet we were no closer to any idea of how our lives should continue.

How it continued : first of all, backward

In September we finally went to the provincial capital Victoria on Vancouver Island. There we liked it very much, but my inner fears kept me from taking even one specific step towards making it our place of living. My wife could not take it anymore and wanted us to return to Germany. This we did on October 3, 2000. And again, we went to North Frisia. There we were occupied with the news about the presidential election in the USA, because at that time I adored Al Gore since I saw in him a hope for a better world. This perception has changed in the meantime, but at that time I could not believe that in Florida he was legally deprived of the presidency due to time constraints during the counting of votes. That was a huge shock for me, and my trust in the political system and the model of democracy was deeply shaken.

More important for us personally was the question of what to do next. We looked at apartments and houses between the North Sea and the Baltic Sea, talked to many people, and still came no closer to a new home. After two months, we gave up there and moved to my brother-in-law in the Rhineland. After a lot of back and forth and with heavy hearts, we then rented an apartment in the town of Siegburg at the beginning of 2001.

In the following two years that I lived there, I was physically present but not mentally, emotionally, and energetically. During all that time, I felt that I had not accomplished my task in Canada, and without this, life could not go on for me. In our flat, I had begun to teach yoga to a small circle of participants, and after a few months our landlord approached me about working in his Edeka grocery stores. I learned that these were located within two correctional facilities, and the work would be limited to 7 days a month. I accepted his offer, as did my wife a little later, and in the following months we got to know the inside of jails. This experience also taught me a lot and gave me insights that only few will be granted. I was moved particularly by the contact with the prisoners and the growing acquaintance with some of them over the course of twelve months in this occupation.

During this time, my wife and I participated in an initiation to reiki, which led me to an intense experience with this form of healing. An astrologer in Kaslo had told me it was my job to work through my hands but these were not yet activated. By means of the reiki initiation, this activation was achieved in a certain way. I think that quite soon, reiki and similar healing methods will be able to replace conventional medicine in most areas.

Our reiki master and her husband also performed family constellations according to Bert Hellinger. We had already gained experience with this, and so I seized the opportunity and brought my desire to return to Canada and face this challenge into a family constellation. During the constellation, my grandfather's role during World War II came to the fore. The family entanglements projected onto me were returned to those responsible, and after the constellation I was able to book a flight to Canada as a preparatory trip for a possible renewed emigration. Until then, I had already made many attempts to fly back to Canada, but insurmountable fears had blocked this every time.

In the meantime, I had quit my job in the prisons and was now working as a cashier and stocker at a Penny grocery store. I had chosen this job because I wanted this experience to prepare me for a possible retail job in Canada. My time at the Penny market really got me thinking. In our store, we were always understaffed for the volume of work we had to handle and always had to do several things at once. It was all due to the customers' unwillingness to pay fair prices for their food, and was also driven by the Aldi principle*. Health-wise, it took a toll on all the employees who worked there. For me it was a valuable experience to meet the colleagues in my store and to

---

* Aldi general stores in Germany do not pay reasonable prices to their suppliers, so that they are able to sell their products at cheaper prices than their competitors.

AWAKENING

get to know the discounter system from the inside. To this day, I would only shop in such a store in an extreme emergency, because I think that people and the production and selling of food should not be treated in the way that happens there or that is forced on producers by price pressure.

During the years in Siegburg, two striking events took place. On the one hand the attack on the World Trade Center in New York in 2001, as well as the final abolition of the D-Mark and introduction of the Euro on January 1, 2002. I believe that these two events contributed very much to the fact that the opportunities of a spiritual awakening and the recollection of extrasensory perceptions were strongly suppressed or even prevented. When I sat at home with the starter kit of Euro coins on January 2, 2002, a deep sadness overcame me and my tears began to flow. This occurrence had a much stronger impact on Germany and its energetics than could be seen on the surface. Likewise, the 9/11 event of 2001 triggered a worldwide traumatization that rolled like a steamroller and took with it the spirituality that had been unfolding since the Harmonic Convergence in 1987, and especially since the late 1990s.

Regarding the events of September 2001, I would like to mention that quite soon after, several hundred architects and civil engineers got together and unanimously stated that the static and structural stress due to the fires caused by the incoming airplanes could never have led to a failure of the structural integrity of the buildings. Also, the buildings would not have simply collapsed as a result of such an event, but would have toppled over. The collapse could only have been achieved by controlled demolition. As well the explanation for the later collapse of WTC No. 7 is not convincing. Supposedly, a fire in the interior of the building led to the total collapse of the whole structure. When metal components were later claimed out of the debris and chemically analyzed, it became apparent that they had been exposed to temperatures that were over double the amount that would have been caused by fires in the buildings. Therefore, something other then aircraft fuel or burning building materials must have caused this high temperature.

Thus, there are many unresolved questions about this issue that severely call into question what happened and the way it was presented. Nevertheless, this narrative remains unchanged to this day, along with the grave consequences that it has on our lives worldwide. Here I would like to encourage you to do some more research on your own.

World events continued with the Iraq war. In 2003, a "Kuwaiti witness" from an infant ward was invited to testify before the U.S. Senate that Iraqi soldiers had removed many infants from her ward and left them out on the street to die. However, this lady did not work in a hospital at all and was the wife of the then U.S. ambassador to Kuwait. She was hired by the advertising agency Hill and Knowlton for this very purpose, because this agency was also responsible for shaping the mood in the USA and among the coalition of the willing for a war against Iraq. Such examples show how in the recent past, which is still very recent for us, interventions were staged and manipulated in order to establish certain grand narratives in the consciousness of mankind.

Canada : lost and regained

At the beginning of February 2003, the time had come for me to travel to Victoria, BC by myself. My research for reasonably priced flights always led me to Seattle, WA instead of Vancouver, BC. Even in later years, flights to Seattle were much more affordable than flights to Vancouver. So, I booked a direct flight to Seattle, WA, arriving early in the evening. From there I took the Bus north to Vancouver, BC, and re-entered Canada around midnight. It felt like — and was for me — a huge accomplishment to having been able to finally come back. After arriving in Vancouver in the middle of the night, I had to wait a couple of hours before the first bus to Victoria, BC left. When arriving there after almost two days of constant travel, I was so excited that I walked with my luggage almost two miles by foot to reach the hotel where I had booked a room.

A good friend we had met at the YDC introduced me to Eckhart Tolle and an audiobook version of *The Power of Now* as well as to the book *Creating Money* by Sanaya Roman during the three weeks of my stay. My friend had me sit in front of a tape recorder during each of my visits so that I could continue listening to Tolle's book. After two weeks, I was ready to take the first steps to build a foundation for making a living in Canada. To do this, I went to the Immigrant and Refugee Center to get advice and coaching on how to prepare job applications and how to go about this process in Canada. During my last visit with my counselor, I made another appointment, even though I would be flying back to Germany before that appointment. What I also learned during my stay in Victoria was that for all immigrants a new ID card would be issued that year, which could only be applied for from within the country and which in the future would replace the original immigration permit as ID upon entry. For my wife and me, the mandatory deadline for applying for this ID card was May of that year. It was clear that if we wanted to return to Canada, we would both have to do so by May.

Back in Germany, my wife and I then decided within a few days that we would try to live in Canada again. To do this, I was going to fly back there just 2 weeks after my return, find a home for us, and take care of all the formalities that were necessary for living there, such as applying for a driver's license and a bank account, and so on. My wife would spend the next two months in Germany unwinding our household and shipping our belongings. During the next two weeks, we went through our possessions which we again reduced significantly. None of the furniture would be taken with us, we were preparing to sell it all. I did not tell my family about my plans, because I was afraid that the solutions found during the family constellation would be undone by them. I had already had this experience after my first family constellation which took place in 2001. The first meeting with my parents after this earlier constellation clearly showed that emotional burdens were indeed redistributed from me to them, but that the previous state was also very quickly restored, *i.e.*, certain family problems and psychological burdens of my parents, presumably from the war and post-war years, were again returned to me. These energies can be passed on from their origin up to seven generations. By means of the family constellation, such passed-on experiences, often traumatic ones, can be returned to the actual people who went through them.

PART 1

Short introduction : Family Constellation

For those who are not familiar with this technique, here is a brief introduction to it.

Family constellations usually take place in a group of 10 to 30 participants. At the beginning of the constellation, the client talks about the topic he wants to set up. This can be persons or circumstances. The leader of the constellation then suggests which family members should be constellated. Thereupon the client chooses representatives for the corresponding family members from the other participants who take part in this event. These can be parents, grandparents, children, siblings, aunts, grandchildren, *etc.*, even those who have already died. It is especially important that the client placing his family members also chooses a representative for himself. Then he places the different family members in a way that currently feels appropriate for him on an area around which all the other participants sit in a wide circle. Once everyone is lined up, the leader of the constellation begins to ask the family members (represented by their substitutes) how they feel. The questions are, for example, whether one feels comfortable in the place where one is, how one feels in relation to the other family members, whether one feels good about oneself, or whether any unpleasant sensations or emotions are present. Now begins a process that can make subliminal problems or conflicts visible. This comes about through the fact that the representatives, who are completely unencumbered regarding the actual family dynamics, all openly address the issues and feelings that they feel. Through targeted further questions of the leader of the constellation, the causes of conflicts or suppressed emotions and topics that have never been openly expressed come to light. By means of appropriate adjustments of the family members, they can be placed into positions in which they feel better. Also, burdens that have been passed on to subsequent generations or other family members can be returned to the actual bearers.

The leader of the constellation rearranges the energetic family constellation, so to speak. And through this rearranging, harmony increasingly returns to the family system. The goal is usually that at the end of the constellation, blockages or psychological and emotional burdens that do not causally belong to the client are transferred back to the respective family members.

The constellation also allows for stressful relationships with certain family members to be brought back to a more harmonious basis. When it is felt that the purpose of the constellation has been achieved, the client enters the new system and replaces his own representative in it. In this way, the client can experience and internalize the solution that has been worked out. If you are interested in this process, you can inform yourself about the work of Bert Hellinger or look for practitioners of this technique in your area. You can usually find them by searching for the keywords "systemic family constellations" and "family constellations."

My flight to Vancouver, BC was scheduled for March 11, 2003. On March 9, I visited dear friends as a farewell, whom I had informed about my plans, and on the night of March 10, I was hit with the worst stomach flu I had experienced up to that point. I could not get out of bed that day and could not take in anything, not even water. Close friends came to visit and looked at me pityingly when I announced that I would still go on my trip the next morning. My brother came over early on March 11, and I left for the airport with my wife and him on shaky legs and completely exhausted. My flight took over 10 hours with a change of planes in Frankfurt, and for the entire flight all I could do was stare at the seat in front of me and concentrate on not feeling nauseous again. I did not eat or drink anything.

Arriving in Vancouver, I had to face the immigration officers in this condition and managed to answer any of their questions before being granted entry into Canada once again. This time, too, it was an enormous step for me, coming here all by myself in such a worn shape and to begin a new chapter of my life, as if having been born once again into this world.

Afterwards I had to survive a 3½-hour bus and ferry ride to Victoria, after which finally my acquaintance from the YDC time picked me up with her car. With the last of my strength and thoroughly cleaned on the inside, at least physically, I made it back to Canada.

PART 1

Within 2 ½ weeks I had my driver's license, a bank account, an apartment, and a job. Even today I cannot believe how I managed to do that. I can still see myself walking for hours from one appointment to another through the constant pouring rain that literally dissolved my shoes.

In my opinion, such an undertaking can only be carried out successfully if it is in harmony with one's own life mission.

Then, on a sunny day, as I looked out from Victoria for the first time at the ocean and mountains across the Juan de Fuca Strait in Washington State, I experienced some of the very few moments in my life where I felt free, lively, and overjoyed.

On April 1, I moved into our new apartment and on April 2, I began working as a sales clerk at a small chain of souvenir stores on Government Street in Victoria. My hours varied from week to week, and I was paid the minimum hourly wage of $8. My hours were distributed over all days of the week, ranging from 8 am to 11 pm, and I sometimes only got one day off per week. Especially the language was a big challenge for me, and the employers did not treat us employees very kindly. There was no holiday entitlement, and if you were sick, you did not get paid. Everything was very different from what it was in Germany at the time. Nevertheless, it was one of the greatest accomplishments of my life that I had the courage to successfully take these steps.

At the beginning of May, my wife had wrapped up all remaining tasks in Germany and was ready to follow me to Canada. She also booked a flight to Seattle, WA, and I arranged for two days off from work to being able to meet her there. From Victoria, there is a fast ferry going directly to Seattle which I took the day of her incoming flight. Thus, after two months of separation, we met at a hotel in downtown Seattle with a magnificent view of the city skyline. It was one of the most touching and joyful moments of my life.

We spent two nights in Seattle and traveled back to Victoria together by ferry on May 9. After we both had gone through immigration again and stood on Canadian soil, tears of joy flowed, and we were finally back were we belonged.

Living and working in Canada, part 1 : getting in and getting out

The following months I was well occupied at work by the summer season, but my feet were giving me more and more trouble. Walking around on the hard concrete floors in the stores did not agree with me, and towards the end of the season in September, after which most of the employees were downsized for the winter, every step hurt. I felt that I urgently needed to find another employment for the future. My employer offered me the opportunity to rejoin them in February of the following year in preparation for the next season, and I accepted for safety's sake. We planned to use the autumn to do some house-sitting with friends in Nelson, BC. We were very drawn to this area, and our time there would tell us if we could find suitable employment opportunities locally. We gave up our small apartment in Victoria, packed all our belongings, including furniture, into a U-Haul truck and went on the 430 miles drive to the Kootenays. On the way we had to pass several high mountain passes. Night fell, and before reaching the last mountain pass it already began to snow heavily in the valley. Never had we driven such a truck and never before had we traveled such distances in Canada in our own vehicle. Nevertheless, we decided to drive on. Through thick snow and deep forests, the route led us to an altitude of over 5,900 ft, and after the clouds broke, we saw a beautiful clear starry sky above us. Ahead of us, the Big Dipper lit the way, and we never forgot this sight. Whenever we see the Big Dipper in the sky, we are reminded of this adventurous journey. We arrived safely in Nelson late at night and stored our belongings in self storage the following day.

However, our time in Nelson made us realize that it would be very difficult to find even part-time employment. In Canada, you need references from previous jobs within the country to have a good chance of being successful in a job application, unless you are a craftsman. Neither of these applied to us. Our finances kept melting away, and after six weeks we decided to return to Victoria in December so that I could resume my previous job there at the beginning of the next year.

PART 1

This time we had to borrow a friend's car to drive over a high mountain pass to a larger town two hours away where we could get a van for our belongings. All this in the middle of winter and through lots of ice and snow. Then we loaded our stuff back in and headed back to Victoria. Despite the long driving time and contrary to our original plan, we spontaneously skipped a second break and kept driving on to the ferry pier in Tswawassen near Vancouver to catch the ferry to Victoria. We were a little surprised at the low volume of vehicles and reached almost without delay a much earlier ferry than we had aimed to.

What we did not know at that time was that the ferry workers union had announced a complete strike effecting all ferry connections, which should start on that very day. And we were indeed on the last ferry to Victoria. After that, the ferry service was completely stopped for several days which had not happened ever before. It was only on the ferry that we learned about this in a newspaper we had bought to look for housing offers. We found an offer that interested us and called there after arrival in Victoria from a pay phone. At this point it should be mentioned that it is very hard in Victoria to get an apartment at all. A halfway acceptable and affordable apartment is very difficult to get hold of. The occupancy rate for rental apartments was close to 99% at that time. Thus, it was amazing that this very conveniently located small apartment was still available at all. The next day we stored our belongings in a self storage again and then went to inspect the apartment. This apartment was still furnished by the previous owner and was in a very unusual condition. Two interior doors were missing, the linoleum floor in the kitchen was disintegrating, the single glazed windows were as old as the building itself, i.e., 100 years, and some of them could no longer be closed completely. Still, we had a good feeling and told the landlady that we would like to rent the apartment. Usually, I cannot really decide on anything so spontaneously, so this was a special occasion from my point of view. The landlady liked us, and we got a lease during this visit which would start a month later. We were lucky, some of the most prominent defects were fixed by the landlady, and the whole apartment was repainted.

AWAKENING

Here, in Richardson Street in Victoria, nine years were to begin, which were so filled with experiences, impressions, and realizations that they could have filled a whole life in my opinion.

The first thing I did was to look around for an alternative to my occupation in the souvenir stores. In the process, I came across a huge call center of the American communications company AT&T Wireless, which was operated by an independent service company founded solely for that purpose in a town 45 minutes by bus north of Victoria. I tried hard to get a job there because I thought it would bring me back to the world of office jobs, which had been my main field of activity in Germany. Despite the requirement that the call center employees (there were about 1,500 there) speak English so well that they could pass for U.S. citizens - and I am German - I got a job. The pay was slightly above minimum wage, and you would get a bonus of 50 cents per hour if you kept your agreed break times and work times to the minute over a certain time period. In addition, there were other strict rules of conduct that you had to follow, and you would also be monitored by quality control staff during your customer talks. The working hours were from 3 pm to 11 pm after a 4-week training period. I did not own a cell phone during all the years in Victoria, but only a laptop not connected to the Internet, which we used more as a substitute for a typewriter. Therefore, this was my most striking encounter with the topic of cell phones up to that point.

In the previous year, I had already wondered why the providers were selling cell phones for $0 for almost the entire year and always kept the first 3 to 6 months of the contract period free of charge. Having owned a cell phone for seven years now, I can understand this sales tactic. The cell phones and digital forms of communication have within a very short time suppressed the development of independent "awakened" communication, such as telepathy, and shifted it to technical devices that are completely controlled and monitored by others. These devices have made mankind addicted to them — and they can be turned off by the providers. On earth there has been a controlled steering of the development and the consciousness of mankind for a long time, in the form of a devolution which constantly restricts the mental and spiritual capabilities in this realm of being and tries to prevent the necessary awakening of mankind.

So, I started my 4-week training period at AT&T and was the only participant in a group of about 20 future employees who did not own a cell phone. To me, all the technical knowledge that was imparted to us was very difficult or even impossible to understand. It was a call center for incoming calls from customers all over the U.S., which meant that we were first trained specifically on the questions and problems that callers usually bring up. Of course, we had to find a quick solution to these problems so that the customer would remain happy and use their phone as much as possible. If the customers were annoyed, we were supposed, after assistance with the problem solution, to generously assign free minutes which pacified the callers fast and reliably and led naturally to their appropriate continued use of their cell phone. The expansion of regular cell phone use is one of the providers' main goals.

What really shook me was the part of the training where we could listen in on the handling of incoming customer calls by the current employees. It became clear to me what an integral, vital part cell phones had become in the lives of people. Because one of the problems that occurred time and again was that the users had not paid their bills, for example, because they simply did not have the money and their number had subsequently been disconnected by the provider. Today, I am in the same boat as the other cell phone users, but back then I was deeply shocked by the catastrophic effects that a cell phone that could no longer be used had on the customers' everyday lives. People were desperate, they cried, begged, and made promises, all just to be able to use their cell phone again. And I understood why the phones had been given out for free including 6 months of no regular payments. After that time, the customers were bound to this device for better or worse and would pay for their next cell phone themselves and at most change the contract from one provider to the other, but no one would do without this device in the future.

After three weeks of training, I felt that my life force was steadily flowing out of me. It became clear that I would not be able to survive in this kind of work and in this industry. So, I quit after 16 days of training. For years, the experience of those few weeks hung over me, and for a long time I was energetically, but also physically, weakened.

Thus, I had no choice but to return to my old job from the previous year directly after the call center experience.

A new history of the universe : Carl Calleman

In the year 2004, again by "coincidence," significant information came to my attention, which explained to me and to my wife why our way of life had developed since 1999 in such an unconventional and for me at that time also incomprehensible way. Until 1999, we were not only quite well off with our respective employers at the time, we also had very good incomes and could afford to live comfortably. Our demands in this regard are not very high, but for us it was natural to have a nice apartment and to be able to attend spiritual workshops whenever something arose that seemed important to us. We were also able to take interesting vacation trips. In the meantime, this had changed dramatically in Canada. We no longer owned a car, we lived in a very small, drafty, and noisy apartment, and otherwise we afforded very little in the way of clothing or eating out. We earned a fraction of our previous income, had only two instead of six weeks annual vacation, no sick pay, and our health began to suffer under the strain of our two jobs. All this gave me more and more food for thought, but at least I had faced life in Canada, courageously accepted all the challenges that came with it, and would continue to do so in the years to come. Nevertheless, at that time I was no longer sure whether it all had a deeper meaning or not.

At that time, it happened that acquaintances of us wanted to start a film club. With three couples we wanted to meet regularly to watch movies together. A first meeting was arranged, but unfortunately there was no film yet. Nevertheless, for me it became a key day regarding the further way towards the ever-approaching moment of awakening. One participant mentioned a book she was reading, which, in her words, explained everything in such a way that she could now understand the meaning of her life and where it was leading. A Mr. Calleman had written it and it was about the Mayan calendar. Her report about this book captivated me so much that I went to a bookstore the next day and looked for it in the order program. The title was: *The Mayan Calendar and the Evolution of Consciousness* by Carl Johan Calleman.

Carl Calleman is a studied biologist from Sweden and was teaching at the University of Seattle, WA at the time. Thus, he lived in our neighborhood, so to speak. Carl was drawn to the Mayan archaeological sites and spent time there every now and then. Even the Mayan natives he encountered assured him that he was not there by accident, but had a mission in that regard. He did not really have an idea what kind of task this should be and had no special insights into the traditions and culture of the Maya. In order to follow his inner call, however, he often stayed at these Mayan sites, sometimes spending a night on top of one of the pyramids. At that time, when the Mayan calendar was being discussed, it concerned primarily the Long Count, which began approx. 3113 BC and according to general computation should end on December 21, 2012. Carl carried out his own calculations, and according to these the Long Count was supposed to end already on October 28, 2011. The Long Count can be divided into 13 sections of time of equal length, which Carl calls 7 days and 6 nights. Carl achieved a breakthrough in his occupation with the Long Count and the Mayan calendar, when he noticed that from the view of the Swedish history, if the Long Count was in a day energy (the Long Count began 3113 BC with the energy of the first day, which changed to the energy of the first night after $1/13^{th}$ of the total duration — ca. 2719 BC) expansive movements always went out from Sweden, such as successful military campaigns and cultural expansions, and during the nights this often turned into the opposite. This discovery was for Carl now the basis of his further occupation with the meaning of the Mayan calendar.

He found out that the Long Count is only reflecting a part of 9 creation waves of the universe, namely the 6th wave. The first creation wave (Carl called these underworlds at that time) began 16.4 billion years ago, and this creation wave also ran through 13 cycles, 7 days and 6 nights, only that each cycle covered $1/13^{th}$ of 16.4 billion years. Each further creation wave vibrated faster by the factor 20, *i.e.*, one cycle of the 2nd wave amounted to only 63 million years, and the entire wave ran over 820 million years. All 9 waves ended on October 28, 2011 or, according to the other Mayan experts, on December 21, 2012.

It is interesting that Carl could derive and exemplify the development of the universe from these creation waves. The first 2 waves with their long cycles were responsible for the development of matter, and afterwards the 3rd and 4th wave began to enable the development of simple life up to more complex mammals. Then from the 5th wave (beginning about 100,000 years ago), the development of consciousness of man took place. Carl further found out that each of these waves sends creative light in different ways to the male and female aspects of creation. Thus the 5th wave was characterized by the fact that this creative light fell equally on the male and female divine aspects. Thereby the people had a unity consciousness at that time, duality had no place in their daily lives. Carl describes it in such a way that people at that time were in a shamanic state of consciousness, that this was their normal state. Also, based on the analysis of works of art originating from this time, he could prove that the earth inhabitants during the dominance of the 5th creation wave could not align themselves into a structured space or imagine such a space. They perceived themselves as existing freely in space. With the beginning of the 6th wave, the cosmic creative light fell on the male side of the brain only, this is the left-brain hemisphere in humans, which favored quickly the rise of the patriarchy and went along with the emergence of the classical religions. However, people increasingly had no longer access to unity consciousness. Duality, together with all the many negative effects we know, came to the fore. Access to the subtle levels, to holistic and connected creation got lost and the world of humans lost more and more the connection to the world of animals, plants, minerals, and in general to the world of elemental beings. Dysfunctionality and a hostile environment left people isolated from the divine.

At the beginning of the 7th wave, about 270 years ago (1755), no light at all fell on creation, and both sides of human consciousness were equally affected by this. In this time, the industrial revolution began as well as the so-called age of enlightenment. A human being was regarded as a random product, living only once, and therefore it made no sense to handle creation with care, since it also represented in its totality only a transient random product. *The consciousness of the 6th and 7th wave represents the dominating energy that shaped the world in which we grew up.*

In 1999, at the beginning of the 8th wave, the creative light fell on the feminine side, represented in the brain by the right hemisphere. Thus, in 1999 a process began which, if it could have unfolded unaffected on earth, could have made possible telepathy and extrasensory perception as well as the reawakening of the connections with creative forces. I say "could have" deliberately. On the 2nd day of the 8th creation wave, there was the "attack" on the World Trade Center, and with this event mankind was put into a shock paralysis. In consequence, on political and technical levels the energy of this wave was directed into other channels. In particular, technical devices replaced the development of telepathic abilities in humanity, and these devices (cell phones and the like) became a tool for monitoring and control of people's consciousness. This was followed by the "war on terrorism" and the introduction of numerous laws to monitor and control people. Through the many social media platforms and the accumulation of all data available about everyone (Facebook, communication via WhatsApp and the like, e-mails, phone calls, Instagram, credit card use, location monitoring via cell phone, *etc.*), digital personalities of each individual can be created in no time at all. And these can be impacted on specifically, e.g., in Internet searches, via radio signals from the transmission towers, but also on a mental level in an energetic way. Anyway, the original creative impulses of the 8th wave could not express themselves adequately in this level of being, and our development out of the 3D world was slowed down. It was interesting for me that I now had an explanation for the radical change of course that my life and that of my wife had taken in 1999. From well paid office jobs in Germany to an ashram in the Canadian mountains within 9 months.

The 9th and final creation wave began on March 8, 2011

and lasted until October 28, 2011 as well. One cycle here comprised only 18 days, the frequency of vibration was unimaginably high compared to the first waves. Right at the beginning of this creation wave, the big earthquake occurred near Fukushima in Japan. Through the following summer, the so-called "Arab Spring" and the "Occupy Movement" took place.

According to his analyses of the effects of the creation waves on earth history, Carl Calleman could prove that new creation waves took over a dominating role in the development and shaping of creation after a certain time following their beginning. This can be proved impressively in particular for the 6th and 7th wave. The 8th wave of creation so far finds its expression mainly in the development and roll-out of the digital information technologies, but not in the further development of human consciousness in relation to the ability of extrasensory perception and a holistic attitude to life. This becomes even clearer with the 9th wave. This wave is characterized again by creation power impacting equally both sides of the brain as well as the male and female aspects. This would mean that duality and the dominance of opposites would have to recede into the background again and a holistic consciousness would have to permeate all aspects of life and being.

And it is the time of awakening, where we become aware of our true being and our origin. Therewith a creation cycle over 16.4 billion years comes to an end. And exactly this is not perceptible in this world which is becoming more and more dysfunctional. Precisely this topic will be the focus of the second part of the book.[†]

[†] I have presented above in detail my understanding of the Mayan calendar according to the interpretation by Carl Calleman. In the last two years, however, I came across new information which severely and convincingly questions the time sequence of the development of earth and civilization as conveyed by conventional sources. Meanwhile I have certain doubts about the assigning of historical events to specific cycles of the various waves of creation. More on this follows towards the end of the first part of this book where I talk about the discoveries of Raik Garve. Nevertheless, the work of Carl Calleman was so significant for my way of understanding that I wanted to present it here in any case.

Since 2012, and although the two highest vibrating waves could not yet unfold to their full presence in our realm of being, Carl meanwhile speaks of the fact that all creative waves continue to run and continue to influence the development of the world. Primarily, he observes the effects of the civilization-forming 6th and 7th waves. However, these should have receded long ago into the background

PART 1

*The nine creational waves of the Mayan Calender
according to Carl Johan Calleman*

Creation-wave	Begin	Duration of cycle (13 per wave)	Creational light on male/female aspects
1	16,4 billion years B.C.	1.26 billion years	both
2	820 million years B.C.	63 million years	male
3	41 million years B.C.	3.15 million years	none
4	2 million years B.C.	150 thsd. Years	female
5	100,5 thsd. years B.C.	7,885 years	both
6	3115 B.C.	394 years	male
7	1755	19.7 years	none
8	Jan. 5, 1999	362 days	female
9	March 9, 2011	18 days	both

Enddate for all creational waves: October 28, 2011

A visit

Before I report on my further professional experiences after my resignation from the call center, I would like to take this opportunity to tell you about an energetic event that took place in the fall of 2004. Whereas my involvement with the work of Carl Calleman inspired and motivated me, this second event burdened me.

As already reported, a family constellation in 2002 enabled me to free myself from my mental paralysis and to orient myself once again towards Canada. I did this without informing my immediate family, as I feared that the energetically liberating effects that the family constellation had brought about could possibly be reversed, as was the case after my first constellation.

In 2004, my mother announced out of the blue that she would visit us in Victoria and that she wanted to stay in our small apartment of 480 square feet, which did not have an extra bed but only a futon which was rather unsuitable as a sleeping place. This announcement and the unwavering consistency with which she pursued it were extraordinary. On the one hand, the fact that she was able to pursue this plan without the intervention of my father (who is extremely thrifty and avoids any unnecessary expense in relation to his immediate

---

with respect to their dominance, and should have been replaced by the lightful energies of the 8th and 9th waves. Here, once again the urgency of the immediate awakening into the qualities of consciousness of these two highest waves of creation becomes clear.

family, although financially very well off) and, on the other hand, that my mother presented us with a *fait accompli* without any prior enquiry, baffled us. I immediately sensed that there was much more behind this visit, and that energetic burdens that had been taken from me during the family constellation were to be returned to me. To this day, I cannot comprehend how my mother managed to implement her plan against the usual reservations and concerns of my father.

With great difficulty, we managed to convince my mother to stay in a hotel and to postpone the time of her visit until after the tourist season, which was very busy for both of us in terms of work. All these concerns did not matter to my mother, she just wanted to join us as soon as possible.

As one can guess, the visit took place, in October 2004. At that time, we both had a strenuous summer of work behind us and now faced the challenge of getting through my mother's visit as energetically safe as possible.

Right at the beginning, she planned to cook for us regularly in our own apartment. The very first attempt ended in a fiasco, because despite our protests, she used the gas oven which contained metal and plastic objects in the bottom drawer. The apartment quickly filled with toxic fumes from the items burning in the drawer, and we were lucky that there was no further damage. Fortunately, I was hereby able to avert the issue of being cooked for and could thus better preserve the privacy of our home.

I think that on the surface, most people will not be able to understand at all what problems I had with my mother's visit. And I can understand that very well. There are energetic levels in life that affect many people but are not consciously noticed. This does not only refer to such smaller incidents, but penetrates our entire perceived world view. More about this in the second part of the book.

We now spent a lot of time with my mother over a period of two weeks, went on excursions, went for walks, she visited us at our work places and of course regularly at our home. On the surface, it was a family visit as it is quite normal and harmless everywhere in the world. But on another level, severe energetic events took place. Quite soon after her departure, it became clear to me that our time in Canada now had an expiration date. I could not foresee when, but I was now certain that it would come. And just as something had happened in the ethereal realm during this visit which had a determining effect on our further life and our freedom, such things happen on many different levels of our individual lives, and in the collective, too. Later, I will come back to the effects this has on the perception of our self, our real being, and our potential.

After my mother's visit, a time began in which I regularly planned a return to Germany, but postponed this again and again for several years.

Working and living in Canada, part 2 : ups and downs

At this point I would like to come back to my re-entry into the souvenir company in February 2004. Almost simultaneously with me, my wife started working there too in another department.

Upon my return, I was offered the position of a merchandise manager for the whole range of souvenir clothing for the meanwhile eight stores my employer owned by now.

While being physically very strenuous, it became in short time my most favorite employment in my professional career. My boss and the staff in my department were great people to work with and I was able to learn a lot of new skills in this special field of retail.

Our main customers consisted of cruise ship passengers from all over the US. All their ships were on a cruise to Alaska and put in a quick stop in Victoria. As their layover was short, most of the passengers opted for a visit of the downtown area so we were being flooded with thousands of customers when the ships were in. As they had only very limited time at their disposal, we as the merchandisers were always busy getting what they needed from our warehouses. I enjoyed getting to know people from so many different states and to learn about their life there. Of course, there were also customers coming in from all over the world which was exciting too.

As we had no main warehouse, the merchandise stock had to be spread through seven different storage locations. Because of the volume of goods that we went through during summer, it became a physically extremely strenuous task to keep up with demand. At some point, I began to realize that I would not be able to keep this pace up for much longer, so in 2005 I began to look for a new employment.

With the help of a former colleague, I was successful in gaining a position at an office supply company. This business operated several retail stores on Vancouver Island and supplied most of the government ministries as well as the University of Victora. So, my expectation was that I might be able to move up to an administrative position at their head office eventually.

I was assigned to one of their retail stores where a new steep learning curve lay ahead of me. Besides all the to me unfamiliar merchandise, I had to train as a postal clerk in their Canada Post outlet. While this was not physically demanding, it became a mental challenge to ingest all the new information in the middle of a very busy work environment.

After 6 months in the new position, I was in dire need of a break so I took the opportunity to help a friend in Nelson who needed someone to look after her cat for a week while she went on a trip.

Right after my arrival there, I began to feel my severe exhaustion. Even after 12-hours of sleeping through, I still felt not refreshed at all. It took me a few days of complete rest to begin recovering some of my strength. The beauty of the Kootenays did the rest and at the end of the week, I was ready to face work life in Victoria once again.

Here follows a small insertion. During the past 27 years, a lot of information was made accessible to me which shows that in the present years, yes, in the present days, we are standing at a universal turning point. A turning point which has never existed in this form before. See also my comments on the encounters with Marko Pogacnik earlier in this book (at the beginning of the chapter "1995 until today : from where to where"). This change concerns beside the earthly level also the spiritual and universal energy levels. Everywhere, the vibration evolves more and more, and certain fields of vibration and levels of existence will no longer be there after this change is completed. The earth in its present form as we know it today will have no more basis of existence, not even as a duplicate, or the like. This form of existence is simply no longer possible in terms of vibration. In order to make this change of humanity possible for all ensouled beings, even to make them aware of it at all, other beings are presently incarnated in human form which were not involved in the development of the earth and earthbound human families so far. And these beings are, regarding their energetic and vibrational form as well as their experience, better prepared for the energetics after ascension than for the energetics of this dying world. Because of this, these beings often find it very difficult to feel comfortable and at ease in the ways of living that make up the existence on this earth. This concept explains to me why "normal" activities and challenges are often so difficult for me and weaken my energy so much.

A few weeks after my vacation in Nelson, an open position at head office in the accounting department was posted, and I took the opportunity to apply for this position. My interview lasted for three hours, and it took another few weeks till finally the message came that my application was successful.

Once again, a strenuous episode began for me. For over six years, I had not done any form of office work and was no longer familiar with the use of regular office software applications. My predecessor had only one week of time to train me on the job before moving on to different position, so the stress level was rising high.

I was faced with learning to handle all necessary skills for my new accounts payable position practically over night, and the continuation of the business depended on the punctual payment of invoices; some suppliers would only ship the next order when the previous bills had all been paid. To top it all off, I was sitting in a tiny office that was located inside the administration building, without any outside light coming in. The ceiling was just 7-feet-high, and through a window at my desk I could only see a dark hallway. During the winter months, I saw daylight on workdays only during my 30-minute lunch break. Every day I struggled with all my might to get this job done, working overtime, and taking work home. The pay was meager, and I knew that in order to continue to have a successful career in Canada, I would have to manage this task satisfactorily so that I would have a positive reference for future job applications. My first month in the accounts payable department was the month with the highest turnover in the history of the company so far. In addition, after 6 months the Windows-based ERP system was changed to an IBM-based ERP system, which I had to manage for the accounts payable department. There was even more overtime, weekend work, and training, and during this time, on my way to the bus after work, I always seemed to feel the echo of thunder inside me, as if explosions had taken place all day. During this time, I also developed tinnitus which has stayed with me to this day.

Besides all this high stress, once again I was able to gain valuable experience.

The software conversion weighed most heavily on me. Practically as a one-man department, I was solely responsible for my field of work in this regard. I had little opportunity to talk about accounts payable to the software expert who had come from New York, since other departments, such as order processing and warehousing, had a much higher priority. More than once I was faced with the situation that after the software change-over, I would no longer be able to pay invoices, with all the consequences this would have for the company. After the new software went online, it happened indeed that no invoices could be paid and no checks be printed. However, we got this under control within a day, to my immense relief.

After 11 months of doing this job, one morning in February 2007, I was standing at our front door on my way to work. My wife said goodbye to me before she left for her job, and I saw her exhausted eyes, one of them quite inflamed. I myself had intense tinnitus and was also at the end of my tether. At that moment, it became clear to me that we could not go on like this, and I said to my wife that we both had to quit our jobs immediately to preserve ourselves, no matter what the impact on our finances. I was virtually determined to return to Germany in the foreseeable future. On the same day, I handed over my resignation to my boss and my wife did the same at her job.

PART 1

New insights and new books

Since I had begun to study the work of Carl Calleman, I regularly read other spiritual books that I came across in the local bookstores. Many of these books dealt with the subject of the shift predicted for 2012. Among them were books about the Hopis, the pyramids and their true age, Atlantis, astrology, books by David Icke, and many more.

Also included was the series of books about Anastasia, published by Vladimir Megre. I had seen these books in bookstores many times, but I had the impression that they were a rip-off. Such thin books, and each of them cost $20. But my dream power taught me otherwise. One night in a dream, I was expressly advised to read at least one of these books. In my dream I was told the number from the book series but in the morning, I could not remember exactly if it was the 3rd or 4th volume, so I bought them both. And I was blown away by the content. So much made even more sense to me now, and my understanding of the interrelationships in this level of existence expanded significantly. Eventually I read all nine *Anastasia* volumes.

And more and more I was led to certain writings and contents. To this day, it feels as if an invisible teacher is guiding me over and over to the next topic which builds on the previous ones.

Anastasia

I do not want to go into too much detail regarding *Anastasia*, but throughout the volumes there were contents that dealt with our inherent potentials, and with the central control of the world by a few beings who operate completely from the background and regularly reincarnate on earth in full consciousness. In doing so, they can immediately pick up the thread from the end of their previous lifetime, unlike the rest of humanity whose knowledge of things like reincarnation and the like has been cast out of them.

Furthermore, *Anastasia* deals with topics like teleportation, telepathy, power of the mind, being in harmony with nature, and much more, i.e., all the topics that have no place in the mainstream (media, schools, universities). Among other things, *Anastasia* lets us know that every human being is entitled from

AWAKENING

birth to a piece of "motherland," without having to pay anything for it, neither for its acquisition nor for its use. This piece of motherland is measured in such a way that it can completely and during the whole year support its inhabitants, usually a family. Examples of this are shown in the books. Usually, a family or a couple takes over their new piece of motherland. The community participates in the construction of the family's new home, and everyone brings certain plants to the garden to start self-sufficiency. All these are planted according to an established pattern. When people lived according to such principles, they had to work only six months of the year for their food supply, during the other six months they were free to devote themselves to any issues that seemed important to them.

For example, Anastasia says that it does not make sense to work in an office in order to earn the money it takes to buy an apple that has been stored and transported for a long time, just to be able to eat an apple. It would take much fewer working hours to grow that apple on one's own piece of motherland. Analogically, this also applies to all other foods. A key role for the cold season is the preservation and storage of a correspondingly large part of one's own harvest.

For their own piece of motherland and the food produced on it, no one demands taxes.

Anastasia also indicates that our view of history does not correspond to the facts, that we are given a false narrative about the development of mankind from the Stone Age to today's supposedly high level.

Prior to *Anastasia*, I had read some books about Atlantis and I also heard about Lemuria. Christa Zettel reports in her book *Die Seele der Erde* (*The Soul of the Earth*) about huge gold mines in southern Africa, which are about 100,000 years old. These are discoveries which do not go together with the conventional narrative about our existence and development. In this respect, the idea was not new to me that we are taught a "story" that is just that, a story. A story that is needed to lock us up mentally in a thought-prison, which ensures that we can be centrally controlled and used, as described by John Christopher and his tripod monsters. More about this later, as I could gain valuable insights about this topic through Raik Garve.

PART 1

I continue now in my chronological narration.

After the termination of both our jobs, I traveled again for a short time to the Kootenays and stayed there with friends. I needed the distance and wanted to explore our chances of finding local employment here after all, which would finally allow us to move to this area. This time, too, it quickly became apparent that the prospects for this were still poor.

Meanwhile, I received a message from my wife that my former boss at the office supplies company had called during my absence. He offered to rehire me at standard market conditions. The reason was that my successor was so overwhelmed with her tasks that she repeatedly did not show up for work and could not be reached on those days, too. A salary in line with the market would have meant a significant increase in pay for me. But it would not have changed the unhealthy workload.

Regarding Nelson, Kaslo and the Kootenays, this seemed to be a hopeless love affair for us. Our hearts pulled us there, but our spiritual guidance did not give the green light, no matter how many times we tried.

I returned to Victoria and we both used the next two months to recover from the exhausting time. We could not yet bring ourselves to return to Germany, and so I began to look for a new employment.

I looked for job offers in private Canada Post outlets. This work requires extensive training and can only be taken on by few applicants right at the start. Also, this complex job is not very sought after by a lot of job seekers. At the time, instead of the $23 per hour paid at Canada Post, the private outlets paid only $9 to $10 per hour, which was just above the minimum wage. For that pay, the requirements were ultimately very high. Since I already had received training for this job through my previous employment, the prospects of getting such a job were very favorable.

I applied for a 2/3 part time position in the postal outlet of one of the larger grocery store chains in Victoria, which is run exclusively by Chinese immigrants, and I got hired immediately after the first interview.

The post office was located in a corner of the supermarket, right next to the entrance to the meat department, where meat was cut, weighed, and packaged on a large scale. Adjacent were huge refrigerated shelves containing the meat products. The heating system, which was supposed to keep the post office warm, did not work for the entire six months I worked there, so it was always very cold, much cooler than comfortable. My shifts ran from 12 noon to 9 pm, and my half-time break was so early in the day that afterwards I had to work straight from 3 pm to 9 pm all by myself. During that time, I was constantly freezing. That was quite a special experience.

Living and working in Canada, part 3 : successes and new insights

During my week in Nelson, a good friend from Victoria had made me aware of a job offer in the Finance Department of the Ministry of Justice. In addition to my other job applications, I had also applied for this position after my return from the Nelson trip and had subsequently received an appointment for a recruitment test and another for an interview.

I noticed that for the rather simple office job that was advertised, you had to present yourself as if you could take over the management of the entire department or division right away. It was expected that you could report breakthrough successes from all your previous employments. In the meantime, this approach has also found its way into the hiring procedures of German companies, and it is often required of the applicant to put on a show more than it is about real potential and competencies. Those who can sell themselves well win. Honesty often takes a back seat.

In this application process, I came in 2nd, so I did not get the job. Later that year, while I had already been working at the post office for a few months, my friend from the ministry contacted me with another job offer in the same department. Once more I applied, and this time there were no internal applicants (they were preferred) but only applicants from the outside. My wife then called me one day at the post office. She had received a call at home telling her that my application had been successful and that I should let them know whether I would accept the job offer.

Up to this point, we had struggled so hard to make a living

in Victoria, had gone through so many fears, challenges, and doubts, and had been so many times at the end of every hope that at this moment we were both up in tears. What seemed impossible had become possible. This position would allow us to continue to stay in Canada for the time being. I would receive excellent health benefits for both of us, including dental and eyeglasses, which we did not have before. In addition, my payment would allow us some financial flexibility for the first time and give us the opportunity to go on vacation together again after 4 years.

Thus began the most pleasant period of our lives in Victoria.

At this time, we intensely followed the cycles of the 8th wave of the Mayan calendar. Approximately every 12 months the energies changed, and much of this could also be perceived from the events in the world, such as the great economic crisis of 2007/2008. I also gathered information about this from many other sources and integrated them into our way of accompanying the energetic development. This included the so-called Lionsgate at the beginning of August (8.8.), a solar eclipse, the summer solstice, as well as portal openings by Solara at special places in the world. Whenever she did this with larger groups, we were energetically present. If worldwide peace meditations were held, we participated in them. The years from 2008 were to be the preparation for the successful conclusion of all the creation waves and cycles. We were in very good spirits. During this time, we also got to know the Oneness University with their Deeksha, practiced by their students. For a short period of time, we were able to regularly participate in Deeksha at a place a few blocks from our home, during which healing and consciousness-expanding energies were transmitted to the participants by the practitioners as part of Deeksha. Guided meditations were being offered as well. We enjoyed this time very much and met some special people.

Besides, I devoted myself intensively to the study of Iyengar Yoga and attended many regular classes. This allowed me to refresh and deepen my training from the year 2000.

Working in the Finance Department of the Ministry of Justice gave me numerous insights into the workings of government, parliament, and democracy.

A special aspect was that British Columbia is one of the very few jurisdictions in the world where service-providing branches of ministries have to bill their services to their clients. Such a branch did not receive its own budget, but financed itself through the services charged to clients. The functioning of our branch depended on the amounts charged.

Due to the global financial crisis, the budgets of all ministries were cut, and the use of our department also decreased. At that time, we had about 140 lawyers and another 100 assistants and research staff. In addition, there were 160 support staff who could not pass on their time to the clients. Thus, we had to cover all our costs through the billable hours of the 140 lawyers and 100 researchers and assistants. As this cost coverage became more and more difficult, and because I had time on my hands since my workload was very small, I developed an analysis tool that made it possible to determine the amount of billable hours per time-keeping employee in relation to their total working time.

By this, our branch became able to make it through this time of financial shortages and I could once again gather valuable experiences.

My wife meanwhile had also found a new job at a large Canadian drugstore chain during this time. There, too, the employees had no regular work schedule, and in the beginning, she was allotted only 10 hours per week so that her income was correspondingly low. Meanwhile, I was able to compensate for this somewhat with my higher earnings. Over time, my wife's weekly hours increased, and our income was now big enough for a little more comfort in life. What proved to be a burden over the years, however, was that I worked Monday through Friday and my wife regularly worked Sundays. As a result, we had no full weekends together for years. She also worked regularly on all stat holidays, except for Christmas day. The beauty of Victoria, the wonderful people, the nearby ocean, the many songbirds, parks, and coffee houses made up for a lot, but not having a 2-day weekend every now and then became a strain.

PART 1

Other important books and their consequences

During these years, it happened that in different ways at the same time three books found their way to me, whose study broadened and deepened my understanding once again. They included the book *Weapons of Mass Instruction* by John Taylor Gatto; the title *Not in His Image* by John Lamb Lash; and the book *Rise of the Fourth Reich* by Jim Marrs.

John Taylor Gatto had been a teacher in New York State for over 30 years, once even Teacher of the Year, and he had advised Senator Edward Kennedy on education issues. Gatto's book dealt with the education system as we know it, who developed it, promoted it, and eventually established it everywhere. And, what purpose it is supposed to serve. I had already read about this elsewhere, but John Taylor has brought this information more to the point in a better and more understandable way, from his own experience as a teacher. Gatto points out that the current education system which all children, for example in Germany, are forced to attend, separates people by intellect and age. It trains the adolescents to be influenced behaviorally by certain sounds (bell for the breaks, gong) and to respect authorities of any kind as an authority of truth or order, *e.g.*, doctors, scientists of all kinds, law enforcement officers, tax officials, politicians, churches, public administrators, *etc*. Also, social models are conveyed which are promoted as being of service to humans and their life. Psychological means are used to prepare people for their role in this society. Other models of society are discredited, and the Western model is highlighted as a prime example. *Weapons of Mass Instruction* describes how children are brought up to be dependent and shaped towards a certain role model. The Rockefeller family has made large investments to help build this education system. In this way they created, among other things, willing people who could be integrated into large corporations as employees and who renounced more and more independence and self-determination in their own lives. People were raised to be useful commodities.

John Lamb Lash deals in his book *Not in His Image* with the Gnostic teachings, which were still very familiar to early Christianity. The title of the book wants to suggest that today's

Christianity does not reflect the spirit of Jesus, but is a subsequently created belief system.

I myself had already dealt with gnostic writings and teachings in the years 1996 to 1999 and had read the scriptures found in Nag Hammadi and Qumran. I admit that I myself often cannot understand the subtleties which are contained therein in a coded way, but it becomes obvious that in the official canonical writings many contents and traditions from the original gnostic writings were excluded. By this, nearly all references were removed from the canonical writings regarding the fact that there is reincarnation. This was common knowledge at that time. Today, the thought of reincarnation is considered heretical. Like so many things, here too one of the great world religions is used as a tool to keep man away from access and knowledge about his real origin and real being and to capture him in artificial thought and world constructs.

In the second part I will revisit the book of John Lamb Lash in relation to the subject of astrology.

The third book, *Rise of the Fourth Reich* by Jim Marrs, which I also read during this time, deals with the entanglements of politics, media, and industry. In his book, Jim Marrs shows how certain families and groups have been controlling for centuries almost all aspects of the world through banks as well as state and government structures. What on the surface looks like independent states, religions, media, or industries is mainly a camouflage and deception that serves to keep people ignorant of the real meaning and purpose of the system behind it. It would go too far here to address all the topics of this book. Nevertheless, I would recommend to deal with the contents of Jim Marrs' work.

If one delves into these topics, it becomes apparent that even the USA is only an artificial construct which was established by forces acting behind the scenes. It is important to keep in mind that the media have been in the hands of a few people for a long time, and that they have formed a unified opinion on fundamental issues. This was true 13 years ago when I read Jim Marrs' book, and it is even more true today when you look at the international mainstream coverage of the supposed pandemic. Even those who believe the mainstream media, would have to ask themselves why there is always talk of conspiracy theorists when it comes to justified criticism of the official narrative. The fact that top-class scientists are raising well-founded concerns is not reported by the so-called quality media. Just as little is written about the consequences of the gene therapy treatments. This is possible due to the programming of the people by education, media, family, and society. Over decades the foundation has been laid, in order to shape the opinion of humans just by use of the media. The crowd is programmed by way of proven and well-developed psychological tools, and when people are asked about their opinion, they repeat without reflection what has been programmed into them via social media, television, radio, newspapers, the Internet, and movies. Independent thinking takes place only within the framework of predetermined narratives that contain a completely artificially created view of the world. Beyond that, in most cases independent thinking does not take place.

It is even inherent in this system that people defend the narratives given to them as true, and they strongly resist explanations such as the ones I have presented here. This is understandable, because we have arrived at this point through great traumatization and have been cut off the memory of our own origin and our very own knowledge. Basically, we have almost no chance to generate knowledge from within ourselves; we are almost exclusively dependent on external sources and explanations. Certainly, in this context the viability of almost all indigenous cultures on all continents has also been destroyed.

My main purpose here is to describe the topics with which I was intensely occupied in those days. It was about the state education system, the gnosis and the contents ignored or suppressed in the Christian teachings, as well as the topic of global control by a few institutions and families.

At that time, I took one of these books with me on my lunch break, which I spent that day in the nearby gardens of St. Ann's Academy in Victoria, BC. It was a sunny and warm day and, sitting on a bench, I took off my shoes and treated my feet to some sun and air. I sat there reading for about 40 minutes before heading back to the office. Immediately after putting my shoes back on, I felt the beginning of a strange pain in my feet. I had owned these shoes for some time and had worn them often. The bench was located on a wide lawn where no dangerous insects were crawling or flying around. Children were playing in the grass and their mothers were sitting next to them.

In the following two weeks, the pain in my feet intensified to such an extent that I could hardly walk. With difficulty I made it to my workplace and wore no shoes there for the rest of the day. If I had to get up in between to go to the printer or similar, it took me half a minute after getting up until the pain in my feet had subsided to such an extent that I could walk a few steps. Neither the ointment "Traumeel" nor insoles or rest helped. I seriously feared that I would end up in a wheelchair, that is how bad the pain got.

By connecting the background of St. Ann's Academy with the books and topics which I had taken there with me for my lunch break and about which I thought there intensively, there appears to arise an explanation to what had happened to me there.

St. Ann's Academy was once a nunnery where children were educated. And at the time of my lunchtime visit, it was the seat of the British Columbia Provincial Ministry of Education. Education, church, and politics. All these topics were exposed and their true intentions shown in the three books I have mentioned above.

While other people may report about their communications with spiritual entities or transmissions and other supernatural experiences, I can contribute almost nothing in this regard. My mind has mostly drowned out all other forms of possible communication, and only through my dreams, especially in the years 1995 to 2002, a lot of important information came to me.

Here in the gardens of St. Ann's, however, there was a powerful reaction from the subtle realms against me, or rather against the topics I was dealing with. Fortunately, nothing similar did happen to me before or after. The pain in my feet lasted for a few more weeks and then slowly disappeared. I never set foot on the grounds of St. Ann's Academy again after that incident, neither with nor without shoes.

In the following years, Barbara Marciniak with her transmissions from the Pleiades, and Barbara Hand Clow with current information about the qualities of time from the astrological point of view and from the point of view of the Mayan calendar, came along as sources of information, as well as Denise Le Fay, to whom I was very grateful for her insights at that time. However, I think that these days she is not able to maintain the clear focus she once had. In particular, from the beginning she took the narrative of a global health threat seriously that began in the spring of 2020. A lot more literature came along, and I remained energetically interwoven with the rhythms of Calleman's Mayan calendar.

Through Denise Le Fay's regular blog "Transitions," I was alerted to the book *Three Waves of Volunteers* by Dolores Cannon. What Denise reported about it sounded very exciting, and so I got this book which turned out to be another milestone in my understanding of the events and developments in our world.

Dolores and the volunteers

Dolores Cannon, together with her husband, was commissioned in the early 1970s to use hypnosis to perform regressions on traumatized veterans of the Vietnam War. The patient was taken back to a point in time before the traumatizing events of the war. In this way, a relief or even healing of the psychological consequences of the respective experiences could be achieved.

Dolores' husband died during the time of this joint work as a result of a tragic car accident. Dolores later continued this form of therapy alone.

In the course of her work, it suddenly happened that her patients no longer traveled back to a point that was in this life and on this earth, but found themselves in situations that no longer had any relation to the world we are familiar with. When the patient under hypnosis was asked about this, his higher self came forward with the information that he had traveled back to a previous existence of the soul which did not take place on this earth. Since Dolores had been brought up firmly in the Christian faith and continued to feel connected to it, it was difficult for her at first to come to terms with such reports and life situations as they were reported in more and more regressions. Nevertheless, during these regressions, it was pointed out to her time and again by the higher selves of the patients that this was exactly where her future task would be. Dolores accepted this assignment and continued her work in this sense for the following 3 decades. In this way, she was able to help numerous people who were struggling with life on this earth to better understand their soul path and to discover their purpose for this life. It also happened more often that, with the help of spiritual forces, physical ailments and afflictions could be healed during these sessions.

Dolores traveled the world and performed these hypnoses and regressions in many places and countries. The treatments were recorded and she began to publish them in books in anonymous form with her own explanations and comments. A book series with the title *The Convoluted Universe* was created. In the beginning, many of the contents were heavily criticized by people from a religious point of view, which led Dolores to be very cautious about the topics she published. In this respect, some of the more relevant issues were left out at first but were then included in later books. These are topics that empower us, but also challenge us to break free from the narrow worldview in which we mentally reside.

The book by Dolores Cannon, recommended by Denise Le Fay, now dealt with an issue that began to run like a thread through the ongoing regressions. Repeatedly there was talk of an impending great change that was to occur in the near future.

Time and again it was reported that earth-bound humanity would not be able to master this transition into a new level of vibration and new level of being on their own. People were meanwhile too caught in their consciousness and too far away from their true being.

For these reasons and in order to help mankind, beings from many planes of existence in the universe incarnated on earth in three waves, during the middle of the last century.

They are star children, who are not involved in the karmic cycles of earthbound humanity and who have brought special consciousness parts which will awaken at the right time, in order to enable the ascent out of embodiment into new dimensional levels of vibration for the earth, humanity, and the other animated existences of life on earth (this includes all forms of existence and appearance, even rocks and minerals).

Regarding this subject, I can also recommend the book *Reign of the Anunnaki* by Jan Erik Sigdell. He also worked with regressions and provides detailed information about the reincarnation cycle of earth-bound souls and how they are caught in this cycle.

I assume that this situation is known to the entities that have been using the earthly plane of being for their own selfish purposes for a long time. Obviously, any direct action against the voluntary incarnations is not possible for these entities, but an indirect one is. The voluntary souls are unfamiliar with the energies and vibrations of the earthly world, and it lies in the nature of their task that they cannot resonate very well with the 3-dimensional life on earth. Especially the voluntary souls who incarnated here at the end of the 1950s and the beginning of the 1960s, are often energetically drained by the harsh and mostly dysfunctional energies they are exposed to, and some have already left this plane of existence. For most of the voluntary souls, it became even more difficult with the beginning of the Galactic wave of the Mayan calendar to assert themselves in social life and especially in work life. The manipulated digital and technical forms of expression that the energies of this wave of creation have taken on in the Earth sphere are not adaptable for the voluntary souls. To me, one of the reasons for writing this book is that this situation is no longer bearable for the star children, both mentally and physically, just as a rubber band breaks when it is overstretched.

To me it became more and more obvious that the developmental leap that was to take place in this time should happen from within and from a largely intact physical plane of existence, as "Ascension in the Body": ascension in physicality and transformation of the earthly plane of existence out of itself. That is why the incarnation of especially prepared souls from many dimensional planes took place. After their own awakening, it will be possible for these beings to accompany humanity on the way to the higher vibrational levels, and thus also the entire life organism of Gaia.

At this point I would like to mention another book, which I had already read for the first time some years ago but which always moved me to deal with it again. *Summer with the Leprechauns* is the title of the book, and the author is Tanis Helliwell from Canada. The content of this book ties in with the information about elemental beings that I took away from the books and workshops with Marco Pogacnik.

Tanis lives in Canada and is of Irish descent. One summer she traveled back to her homeland and lived there for a few months in a small secluded cottage. During this time, she encountered beings from the elemental world. Tanis shares in her book many of the experiences she had at that time, and some of the knowledge that the elemental beings imparted to her. Among other things, she talks in detail about her insights into the work and the tasks of the elemental kingdoms existing in all earthly elements. It becomes clear once again that the suppression of knowledge about the elemental beings and their tasks from the consciousness of humanity played a key role in the creation of the dysfunctional living world known to us. Important issues here are the sudden "necessity" to use fertilizers and pesticides in agriculture, or the enormous effort it takes to produce objects that mostly have an unsatisfactory functionality and durability. Furthermore, people's health is degenerated significantly by the displacement of elemental beings from their functions. The belief systems conveyed to and energized by mankind banish the elemental beings to a large extent from our realm of experience. This lack of energetic support has made possible the forms of society known to us, which are determined by an unmanageable flood of supposedly necessary work because people now must cover tasks for which they are unsuited without the support of the elemental beings.

Tanis was apparently also told that the most fundamental information she received at the time would not be allowed to be shared with people until about ten years after her book was published. Unfortunately, these contents have not been published to this day.

To me it is important that we must urgently and as soon as possible become aware that we are interwoven in manifold life processes, much more complex than we can even begin to imagine. For example, the existence of our present plane of being would not be possible without the work of the elemental world. The world of elemental beings is very dependent on the mental state of human beings. The more people behave in a way that is disconnected from nature, and the more the natural worlds are manipulated and destroyed, the less the elemental beings can fulfill their tasks. For example, genetically altered organisms no longer have an image on the elemental level. However, this is necessary for their holistic energetic development and for the infusion with the creative power of biological organisms. Genetically modified food largely lacks those components that are necessary for the maintenance and supply of the subtle bodies of man.

The elemental beings need the consideration and respect of humans, because they fulfill a key role regarding the ability of spiritual entities to enter physical manifestations, e.g., that our soul can exist in our body. On the current path to transhumanism, this interconnection would be destroyed and the soul would become only an empty shell, with its divine light severed from it. While this agenda continues to progress, we humans are truly and literally discussing ourselves to death, in spiritual circles as well.

The Inner Earth and the Journey to Mount Shasta

Another remarkable development began when my wife gave me a book by Dianne Robbins on the subject of a hollow earth, *Messages from the Hollow Earth*, for Christmas 2009. At first, I had no idea what to make of this topic, I had never heard of it and I thought that living spaces below the earth's surface were completely sprung from the realm of imagination. Since I nevertheless wanted to adequately appreciate this gift, I read this book by Dianne Robbins.

And it captivated me. Dianne told of expeditions undertaken by the American military to the North Pole, and of mysteries related to entrances to the inner earth that are said to be located at the poles. This indicated at least that these entrances were known about in small elite circles but, like so many things, were kept out of the public eye.

AWAKENING

Dianne has and had for many years spiritual contact with beings from the inner earth. Many of these beings are obviously descended from the Lemurian and partly from the Atlantean civilization. What especially impressed and touched me in Dianne's report were the descriptions of life in the inner earth. All living beings are treated respectfully, also the ground on which one walks is treated with love and consideration, and the number of personal possessions is kept on an absolute essential level. Objects that are needed are made according to the criterion of maximum durability, and when the owner no longer needs them, they are left for others to use. I was so touched by the descriptions and reports that I looked up the location of the famous Mount Shasta, under which there is supposed to be a Lemurian city. On a map showing the Pacific Northwest, which I had purchased shortly before, I saw that Mount Shasta was at the southernmost end of the area covered by the map. At the northern end of the map was our home town of Victoria. I felt strongly drawn to this place, and in January 2010 I suggested to my wife that we travel there in April, to California. She agreed and I started planning our trip. For this trip we had only one week vacation, and because of the long distance I had to schedule stopovers. My wife read a lot of travel guides in order to be able to visit the most beautiful sights along the route, which would take us through the US states of Washington and Oregon.

On April 10 we began our trip, which turned out to be so different from what we had imagined. For the trip, I rented a car and we took the Coho Ferry to Port Angeles in the US state of Washington. From there we drove south along the Olympic Mountains and into the state of Oregon, past the city of Portland and on to Corvallis, where we spent one night. The following day, our route took us through the fertile Willamette Valley and the city of Eugene into southern Oregon to Ashland. I was familiar with this place because it is the home of the well-known author Neal Donald Walsh, who wrote the book series *Conversations with God*. I had already read the first volume of this series in 2000, and later other books from the series from which I took some very interesting thoughts. I asked myself how it could be that the contact to God, who regularly spoke to people in biblical times, suddenly broke off 2,000 years ago and that nowadays one can only get in touch with God through the texts found in the Bible. No priest, not even the pope himself, could add new chapters to the Bible with current messages from God. And then, Neale simply takes a pencil and a note pad and asks God for a dialogue. Interesting what came out of that. And surely each of us could try this as well, to turn directly to God with the important questions of life in general or related to our own life.

We spent an hour in Ashland, had a meal and drove on in pleasantly mild early spring weather towards California. Mount Shasta is on the 41st parallel north, so I expected spring-like weather by mid-April, at least in the town of Mount Shasta. The community is located at an elevation of 3,600 ft., and the average daily highs for April there are 68 degrees and the average lows are 54 degrees. Now that we had arrived in California, the weather deteriorated visibly and it began to snow. The snowfall became heavier and heavier, and when we finally arrived at Mount Shasta Resort after some searching, there were already 4 inches of snow on the ground.

I did not let the weather stop me, and late in the afternoon I happily trudged through the snow to a hot tub across from our cabin. In the evening, we ate spaghetti and looked forward to our trip to Redding, CA which was planned for the following day, where it should be warmer with some Californian flair. Alas, it did not come to that anymore. Only two hours into the night, I was hit by a stomach flu that even exceeded the intensity of the one I had in 2003. My body revolted for several hours, and by morning my digestive tract was completely emptied. I could hardly stand on my feet. My wife was similarly affected, but not quite as drastically. We could barely leave our cabin on that day, and on the following days we had only enough strength for shorter trips into the village and the closer surroundings. Higher up the mountain we also could not get, because there were still huge amounts of snow. What we did, however, was to fill up some large bottles with water at the source of the Sacramento River, which springs from Mount Shasta. Thus, we were able to drink this special water, of whose miraculous effects there are many stories, for several more days. We recovered only slowly from this episode and were still very tired when, after four nights, we started on the very long return journey of 600 miles. For an intermediate stop in Depoe Bay, OR, we had rented a beautiful room with its own outdoor jacuzzi overlooking the Pacific Ocean, but unfortunately could not use it due to our weakness. Still, it was one of the most beautiful drives we have had so far. The following day, we continued to the Juan de Fuca Strait to Sequim, WA, and meanwhile we felt much better.

It was certainly no accident that had led us to Mount Shasta, and the on-site experience probably had its own special reason. My feeling has long been that in our travels and the special places we visit, we gather the ingredients and experiences that prepare us for the ascension and awakening that is just around the corner. And on that journey, Mount Shasta holds a key role for my wife and me.

The Mayan Calendar and its end

Soon the special year 2011 would finally begin, in which on March 9th the last and most momentous wave of creation of the Mayan calendar would start. For us it was this year on which we were focused, the year which according to my expectations would bring us into our power and reveal the real meaning for our being here, the year which would lift the veils from the consciousness of mankind and flood our earth, and not only the earth, with love and light. And I initially wanted to write my book already at that time, as a documentation of the path that my wife and I had walked together up to that point, and as a guide for all those who feel that something very special is in the air, that the pinnacle of all life is imminent and that we may all participate in an unimaginably beautiful cosmic gift.

For this beginning of the Universal wave of creation, we rented a car that was only equipped with summer tires, and drove from the beginning of spring in Victoria towards Nelson, BC and right into winter. We had underestimated that in the mountain world and on the mountain passes of Highway 3 there was still deep winter. However, Canada is prepared for such conditions and fortunately our route was well cleared of snow and ice. In Nelson we stayed overnight with our friends.

PART 1

To welcome this 9th wave of creation, we drove to the ashram where we had completed our yoga training in 2000. The residents there listened with interest to my story about the special nature of these days, and we brought the ideals that the 9th wave stands for into their evening Satsang: unity consciousness, connectedness, enlightenment, love for all creation, and truth. My wife and I used these days to tune into the coming months in our own way, and in the spirit of Swami Radha.

The strong earthquake in Fukushima on March 11, 2011 showed the beginning of great and dramatic changes; the Arab Spring and the Occupy Movement seemed to indicate that a new creative energy was making itself clearly felt in the human world. We felt confirmed in our focus by these events and took the opportunity again and again to tune into the flow of energy, especially at the start of each of the seven day-cycles of the universal wave that began every 36 days (remember, each of the 13 cycles of this wave — 7 days and 6 nights - lasted 18 days).

When we heard about worldwide synchronous meditations, we participated in them, and in September we went again to the Kootenays to our friends in Nelson for two weeks. This time and its great promise filled us with confidence, vitality, strength, optimism, love, and joy, in fact with all fine and positive emotions imaginable. Today, when I look at photos from that time, we both radiate these energies everywhere.

The weeks passed and the excitement and enthusiasm grew. We accompanied the day of the completion of all 9 waves of creation on October 28, 2011 (according to Carl Calleman's calculation) by staying in a small bed-and-breakfast north of Victoria on the Saanich Peninsula. We had with us the books on the Mayan calendar and some gifts we had received from my brother-in-law and his wife.

In his interpretation of the Mayan calendar, Carl pointed out that the Great Pyramid of Chichen Itza in Mexico, with its 9 steps, symbolizes the creation path of the 9 waves. When the 9th wave (step) is completed, the world has entered its perfected state, and the god Quetzalcoatl descends from the 9 steps into our plane of being. I imagined this as the divinity becoming visible in this world. Expectantly, we fell asleep on the evening of 10/27, full of anticipation of everything beautiful that would come the next day.

And then a day began for us that felt not at all different from the days before. No nocturnal dreams had inspired us, the world went its usual course on the outside. We had breakfast at the host's house and decided to go to a nearby butterfly garden for some inspiration, a lovely oasis of beautiful tropical plants, butterflies, and exotic birds.

Inside there was also a glass case in which butterfly pupae were attached to rods. I noticed that a butterfly was in the process of breaking free from its chrysalis. Ever since my training in dream analysis, the transformation of a caterpillar into a butterfly has been a powerful symbol of transformation for me.

So, I lingered to observe the completion of this butterfly's transformational process. It struggled to free itself from its chrysalis and jolted restlessly on the rod to which its chrysalis had been attached. It simply did not come to rest to give its wings time to dry.

To make matters worse, the butterfly lost its grip on the rod and fell onto the blotting paper 12 inches below. Its still wet wings stuck to it, and the precious liquid from the wings which still had to harden, was absorbed by the paper.

Shaken and frozen I stood there, and the feeling that on this day the expected transformation of the world would not happen became stronger and stronger. The butterfly symbol was a powerful message in this regard.

Of course, something did happen at that time. However, and I will come to this in more detail in the second part of the book, the negative forces, which during the previous waves of creation (especially the 6th and 7th wave) have controlled the events on the 3D earth and in the 4D world, where the souls of human beings stay between their incarnations, had also prepared for this moment for a long time.

The ascent of our earthly world into a new level of vibration is to take place in a way that makes it possible for this to happen during the incarnation. As can be learned from the traditions of the native peoples of the earth, e.g., the Hopi, previous worlds regularly came to an end with various kinds of catastrophes, be it floods, conflagrations, or the like. Thereby also the biggest part of earthly life was regularly destroyed at the same time.

However, as Dolores Cannon has already worked out in her above-mentioned book, this time the change into a higher consciousness is to take place from humanity itself, and the voluntarily incarnated souls will thereby open the doors in our consciousness which are necessary for our ascension.

Remark

I did not find any satisfying explanation by Carl Calleman about what in fact had or had not happened on October 28, 2011, and afterwards. Therefore, I share here my personal feeling about it.

Indeed, the 9 cosmic waves of creation found their completion on this day, their highest form of expression. With it, a state occurred which has not existed at least in the previous 16.4 billion years. Thus, an entire creation potential in its highest form of expression was now available at any time. And from the cosmic point of view, a world like the one in which we had been until then was no longer supported energetically, a world that was dominated by the energies of the 6th and 7th waves of creation.

What we experience, however, is how well the beings that dominate the earthly plane of being have prepared themselves for this moment. Highly vibrant creative universal energies are now available, but the manipulated world view created during the 6th and 7th waves has been maintained in all its dysfunctionality by the "synchronized" spiritual creative power of humans. This synchronization had been made possible through various methods of mind control over thousands of years. We were collectively manipulated into an artificial view of the world which we believe in, which we have internalized, and thus together create into reality day after day. And this manipulation is rapidly developed further these days in such a way that we are completely destroying our living sphere, not only on the 3D level, but also at least on the 4D level. In order to build a bridge for human souls into the 5D-realm and higher, it is now necessary that the voluntary souls remember and live their mission in every form.

AWAKENING

My wife and I had already signed up in advance to participate in a spiritual gathering on the occasion of the 11:11:11 (November 11, 2011), and despite our disappointment at the time, we still wanted to commit this moment. The 11.11.2011 was the date mentioned in Solara's book, i.e., universal vibrational levels should have partially overlapped by then in order to make the transition possible from one level (3D level of this world) into a higher level of existence (e.g., 5D).

As described above, Solara started preparing for this in 1987 with a big ceremony at the Cheops Pyramid in Egypt. At this ceremony, Gabriole Springford from Vancouver Island was also present. She has kept the 11:11 energy going over the decades in multiple ways. Gabriole channels various spiritual entities and works with crystals, including the famous crystal skulls some of which she guards.

On November 11, 2011, as in the years before, a big meeting of like-minded people took place near her home, people who wanted at this moment to open the gates between the worlds, in order to make the vibrational ascent of the earth and mankind possible. At the same time Solara, who had moved to Peru in the meantime, organized a ritual which was carried out by her followers simultaneously in every time zone of the world. This, too, served to anchor the new and higher vibrational energies on the earth plane.

So, on the evening of November 10, 2011 we drove from Victoria to Nanaimo, BC with a rental car to participate in this ritual.

The next morning, we dressed mostly in white as recommended by Gabriole, and went to the place of the gathering. A labyrinth of crystals had been set up in a hall, at the head of the room was a large clear crystal skull, and interspersed in the labyrinth were other, but smaller, amber crystal skulls. Also at the head of the room was a pyramid made of copper rods. We had already experienced a lot, but the energy we encountered here was so intense that it took a lot of strength for us to stay there. Almost all the other participants had taken part in similar gatherings before and were much more familiar with the crystal energies than the two of us.

Very special of course was the first 11:11 moment of the

day at 11:11 in the morning. We all walked one after the other through the crystal labyrinth, and each had a private moment with the big crystal skull in the copper pyramid. Afterwards, one of the participants brought very large and high crystal bowls into acoustic vibration by means of a wooden staff. The energy in the room was charged many times over, and I am sure that there was a lot of movement on the subtle etheric levels.

We stayed there until early afternoon, then there was a longer break until it was time to continue in the evening. However, we decided to spend the evening in our room and to have our own little ceremony at 11:11 at night.

Even after this day we did not notice any perceptible changes in the world. Like our feelings after October 28, 2011, we were quite depressed after November 11, 2011, because in a world that continued in its dysfunctionality without change, we no longer had a vision for our future lives.

But then, December 21, 2012, assumed by most as the end point of the Mayan calendar, was still ahead, and we now directed our focus on this date. A possible return to Germany also moved more and more into the center of our considerations.

Canada says goodbye : Germany says hello

I was not really thrilled about the idea of returning to Germany, and I tried for months to find a more suitable apartment for us in Victoria. In our mailbox we had found an extensive letter from a law firm, which was intended for our landlady but was addressed succinctly to the tenants of the house, since the lawyers apparently did not know her exact address. This letter was about the fact that our landlady had obviously not met her installment payment obligations and was told that if she continued to be in default, her house, in which we also lived, would go into foreclosure. At that time, the landlady lived in a lower floor suite of the house and had no public letter box and no name plate.

When I asked the lawyer what the foreclosure would mean for us as tenants, I was told that we would have to move out at fairly short notice. Given the occupancy rate of rental housing in Victoria, that was a very frightening prospect.

But as much as I ran from one apartment viewing to another, often together with my wife, it was alarming to see that we would have to pay many hundreds of dollars more in rent for worse apartments, such as in the basement, or right next to a gas station. One apartment was located on a through road which was so noisy that communicating in front of the house was only possible by almost yelling. Thus, we put our focus toward Germany more and more.

And I learned that it is not so easy to return to Germany after almost ten years of absence. I had to find a health insurance that would take us back, and organize from afar the purchase of a car through my brother.

In the middle of the year, it became clear that we would be going back at the end of September/beginning of October. I looked for a furnished vacation apartment in Siegburg and the surrounding area because we had lived there for many years before emigrating, and there I hoped to have the best prospects of successfully making a new start in Germany.

With a (supposedly) very good-humored host and his wife, I finally found and rented such an apartment for 2 months. I organized the health insurance, transferred bit by bit our Canadian dollar balances to our German bank account, and looked for a freight company that would ship our possessions that we wanted to take with us to Germany. This all worked out relatively well. Once again, we gave away over half of our possessions, all of it as donations.

What I found remarkable at the time was that I had no doubts or fears at all about returning to Germany. I felt driven out of Victoria by strange spirits.

For me, it is very unusual not to endlessly think back and forth about such a decision, and not to endlessly play through in my mind all the eventualities of what might not work out after our return. None of this took place, and that was nearly the only time in my life so far that it happened to me like that. For many weeks, we sorted out things we did not want to take with us and took them to various recipients. It became an enormously exhausting experience together with the packing of the moving boxes.

PART 1

At the end of September, we moved into a hotel for a few more days, and on October 2, 2012 we flew back to Germany.

On October 3, our new landlord picked us up at the train station in Siegburg. Up to this point, I was still in very good spirits.

His wife had cooked for us, and they brought the meals to our apartment in the evening. However, they took the opportunity to shower us with an unexpected wave of negative information. Among other things, they said that basically there was no possibility of finding any kind of employment in this area, and if there was, it was totally underpaid. In this style it went on for more than half an hour, and they really pulled the rug out from under my feet. Exhausted by the long journey and with the feeling that I had not really arrived yet, this negative torrent of words found its way deep into me without any protection and left me depressed and desperate.

From that moment on, I was not sure whether to stay, or whether we should return to Canada right away, even though we could not have regained our footing there so easily, and the effort would have been enormous, of course. Nevertheless, from that moment on I was afraid of our future in Germany. And this fear became even greater, after several meetings with friends and relatives began to sober me up about our supposed prospects. The Germany we had left ten years earlier no longer existed. This became painfully clear to me, but the people in Germany seemed not to have noticed this extreme change.

While I had not yet fully swung back into the German energies, I noticed, for example, how in the preceding decade many regular and permanent employment contracts with the actual employer had been replaced by temporary employment models. Employers no longer made any commitments to their employees but had them on loan from third parties, so that they could terminate using them at any time from one day to the next. For the people in Germany, this change had apparently taken place so gradually that they had not noticed it so clearly. Nevertheless, life loses quality when, on the one hand, you are paid less than before and lose all job security, and on the other hand, you must be available at any time to work within a large area around your home in order to meet the requirements of the employment contract with the temporary employment agency. In the beginning, I was particularly struck by how haggard and stern the German women looked. I could read this energetic tension in their faces. As the months went by, I no longer noticed it, because it seemed now a normal condition for me as well.

What I also noticed was that the numerous esoteric shops that existed at the end of the 90s, where semi-precious stones, spiritual books, yoga accessories and other items were sold, had almost disappeared. Also, the offer of spiritual workshops and courses had severely decreased. I had expected that the opposite would be the case in the years towards 2011/12.

I found it difficult to cope with all this, and my state of mind increasingly deteriorated. However, the weather, which was extremely fine for October, helped. Lots of sunshine and temperatures that regularly rose above 65 degrees and a few times even above 70 degrees allowed us to spend a lot of time in nature.

Our search for a suitable apartment turned out to be difficult. This was especially due to the fact that we had no jobs and no other regular income. Finally, we found landlords who considered accepting us as tenants. However, in order to get the apartment, they asked us to pay the rent for the following 24 months in advance, in addition to the 3 months deposit. Furthermore, we had to disclose our financial situation and hand over copies of our current account statements, which was not easy for me.

I still remember well the invitation to a longer conversation with our potential landlords, in which they questioned us extensively about all aspects of our lives. My panic grew; I had the feeling that I was falling into a trap from which I would not be able to escape. While I usually take the lead in such matters for both of us, this time it was my wife who stepped into the breach. I hung on her calm voice with my whole being, and it is only thanks to her that I did not jump up to leave the house hastily. In the end, the conversation was successful and we received a rental contract starting December 1, 2012.

PART 1

A lighthouse, the Lembecksburg, and a children's home

For the month of December, I had already booked a vacation apartment for us on the island of Föhr, as we wanted to spend there the 12/12/21 and before that also the 12/12/12 and accompany it energetically.

At the beginning of December, we moved everything that we did not want to take with us on our trip north out of the vacation home in Siegburg to our new place. The only pieces of furniture we had received so far were 2 slatted frames and 2 mattresses, the rest was still on order from various furniture stores.

On December 6, we started our journey which would lead us first to my parents who lived near Bremen. Right at the beginning, a large flock of cranes flew over us on their journey to the south, which I found very moving because December is already very late for these birds for their long migration.

As soon as we were on the highway heading north, it started snowing harder and harder. It became a difficult and exhausting drive through hours of snowfall. Exhausted, we arrived at my parents' house in the afternoon. We had not seen my father in over 10 years and my mother not since 2004. The visit was friendly and uneventful.

Two days later, our journey continued to Dagebüll in North Frisia. After we passed through the Elbe tunnel, the gates of heaven opened and it poured in torrents from a gloomy dark sky. It was again an exhausting ride that would also take us through the town where I grew up in the 70s. We had a late lunch there, and as we drove on, temperatures began to drop steadily. After the day's heavy rains, the wet ground quickly froze over, and we had to drive carefully and yet try to get to our hotel in Dagebüll before nightfall. We made it with the last of daylight, and the next morning icy east winds blew in even colder air. These winds gained so much strength in the following days that the ferry service had to be canceled again and again, as the waters of the Wadden Sea were blown out into the North Sea. But we still managed to get to Föhr on schedule.

The next challenge awaited us in the booked apartment.

AWAKENING

The landlady told us right at the beginning that her husband suffered from a severe and fatal lung disease and that there would be frequent and prolonged coughing fits at night, which unfortunately could be heard in all rooms. A great tragedy lay over the whole house.

After the weather had not been kind to us the entire way here, and the previous 2 months in Germany had cost me a lot of strength, I was no longer up to the situation. However, the landlady had already taken precautions, as she had expected that we would possibly not be able to spend the next 3½ weeks under these circumstances, and we got a quiet vacation home a little outside the town of Wyk with another landlady.

After the sobering experiences on October 28 and November 11, 2011, it was important for us to direct all our focus on the alignment of our solar system with the galactic center on December 21, 2012 and, together with the many millions of people who were preparing for this day, to make a renewed effort to bring the divine light and the divine truth to our earth.

First, however, we wanted to celebrate the 12/12, which was seen by many people as the gate opener for the energetically high vibrational time until December 21. For this purpose, we took the ferry from Föhr to the island of Amrum, where the 138 ft high lighthouse was open as an exception due to the calm weather on that day. We climbed the lighthouse and used a quiet moment to celebrate a small private ritual up there, inviting the divine light into this plane of being. The view from above seemed otherworldly, and through the cloudy sky the sun kept shining with a glistening aureole. Those minutes felt very moving, and we were grateful to be able to mark this special moment in such a beautiful manner. For the rest of the day, we walked around the island, looking out over the North Sea again and again. We found back to our own center quite a bit and were able to tune into the coming weeks.

So far up north, days in December are very short, and so we spent a lot of time in our apartment and used the opportunity to get back to ourselves and to find distance to the previous exhausting months.

On Föhr, we had chosen the remains of the Lembecksburg as the place for the 2012/12/21. From there, we wanted to take part in the worldwide coming together of like-minded people for this moment at 11:11 am CET (that was the time at which the earth should be exactly aligned with the center of our galaxy). We visited this place in advance to check out the lay of the land. All that is left of the Lembecksburg is a very large ring wall, completely overgrown with grass. We decided to perform our own ritual inside this rampart on December 21.

Following our trip to Amrum, the weather began to deteriorate steadily. The icy eastern winds increased, and it snowed repeatedly and some times we had freezing rain. It was almost impossible to stay outside on some days, and the weather was unusually cold and snowy for an island in the North Sea. Nevertheless, we explored Föhr on several hikes and visited the grounds of a children's home, where I had spent a 6-week cure almost 50 years ago. Here it was my intention to suffuse the events of that time with healing energies.

At the beginning of the 70s, I frequently suffered from a spastic bronchitis. This caused me to be bedridden for 5 to 10 days at a time with severe coughing and breathing difficulties, and the family doctor regularly made house calls to treat me. As this began to turn into a chronic condition, the family doctor recommended that I be sent to the island of Föhr for a 6-week cure, alone and without my parents.

Nowadays, there are some rather unfavorable reviews of these children's homes, which were probably not always conducive to the psychological well-being of the children. I, too, have some unpleasant memories of this time. For example, my body weight was regularly checked, and I was repeatedly told that if I did not gain weight, I would have to stay there for another 6 weeks, which caused increasing panic in me. Then I caught a severe cold that left me alone in the infirmary for a week. They took away my camera during this time, which I never got back, and my letters home were censored, so I could tell little about these occurrences to my parents. My stay there traumatized me in some ways, but fortunately my bronchitis later improved.

I think that through my revisit there, I was able to bring that experience to a loving healing.

AWAKENING

On December 21, 2012, icy winds blew again from the east as we set out in the morning to celebrate this special moment at the Lembecksburg, together with the many other people who gathered around the world for this occasion.

We stood alone in the wide round of Lembecksburg at 11am, wrapped in heavy jackets and braving the wind. A small pond had formed in the center of the old castle complex, otherwise the damp ground was overgrown with medium-high grass, and in some spots, there were remnants of snow. We felt lonely there, two veterans who had come a long grueling way and who once again poured their hearts, trust, love, and faith into this, into a moment of shared hope for the awakening of this world.

During our time in Canada, we were taught the Divine Light Invocation ceremony at the ashram. Over the years, we had done this invocation at almost every place we had traveled to. And now inside the Lembecksburg too, we started such an invocation a few minutes before the exact alignment of the Earth with the center of our galaxy. During this invocation, we connected the place where we were standing with all the other places on Earth where people were celebrating this moment. We flooded Gaia and all her inhabitants with light and finally imagined the earth lifted into the all-embracing divine being and divine light. Afterwards, we stood silently in the wind, filled with hope and happy to have made it this far together and to have remained true to our spiritual path.

Later, we discovered an old farmhouse in the nearby village of Nieblum, which in the meantime housed a small company that sold healing teas and semi-precious stones. In the fairy-tale-like interior, there was a corner that was prepared as a tea room. We sat there all by ourselves, only a cat kept us company. There we warmed up and listened to our inner selves, letting the moment we had just experienced sink in.

Again, this time too we could not notice any visible changes in the world. Christmas was coming, and every day the island was filling with more tourists who wanted to spend the Christmas season there. Wyk, the main community on the island, turned into a lively town, all the stores were open, even the cinema center resumed its operations for those weeks. Life went on as usual, and hardly anyone had taken notice of the special day of December 21.

For 17 years now, my wife and I had been preoccupied with esoteric, spiritual, and metaphysical issues. We had not felt comfortable in a conventional life for a long time, and in our hearts, we felt that an awakening into the light, into the realization of one's own true being for the sake of humanity and the earth was pending, so that we could all together move further and further towards a holistic and harmonious existence, in synchronicity with creation. And yet we were now faced with the task of rebuilding our lives in Germany in 2013 after more than 9 years of absence. It was to be a huge feat, which eventually would lead us far away from our ideals and hopes. All our energy was needed to find our way back into the German work life. In the process, our spiritual ambitions retreated further and further into the background.

First however, with the help of our remaining savings, we flew for 3 weeks to the Canary Island of La Palma, since our furniture would not arrive until the end of January. On La Palma, the profound emotional and physical exhaustion that had built up over the past few years really emerged. We were very grateful for this opportunity to rest. Nevertheless, we literally fell to our knees there. Each of us fell once on various hikes, and our guardian angels saved us from further harm. It makes a difference if on the one hand you continue to perform your tasks in 3D society in full, and on the other hand, without always being specifically aware of it, you are energetically involved in the change of the worlds. The latter is not measurable and hardly explainable, it costs however much energy and strength. And exactly the effect of this was what we experienced on La Palma.

After our return to the new apartment, winter moved in. Exactly in that year it was bitterly cold until the first week of April. Our new place of residence was located 650 feet above sea level, and we had the feeling that we had moved into the mountains, as it snowed there so much and so frequently. Two months began during which furniture arrived regularly and our new home took shape. We also received our boxes from Canada with the remains of our household goods, via England.

Already in Canada, I had planned to continue my education by taking a correspondence course to become a certified accountant, as I wanted to update my professional background after being away from Germany for so long. Thus, I started a 7-month full time home study program in June 2013. In January 2014, I passed my final exam and from then on, I was looking for a suitable employment.

Barefoot shoes : pleasure and pain

In the meantime, my wife had obtained employment again with her former employer, despite a 14-year absence from any type of office work. It was to be much more difficult for me to find a new job, despite my further education. I sent off 21 job applications between February and May 2014, even selecting basic jobs with low incomes, but I did not receive a single response, not even a rejection.

Then I discovered a job offer at a company that sold Barefoot shoes. I had never heard of this company before, but it was easily accessible by bus, and the job comprising order processing seemed very feasible to me. In addition, at that time I began increasingly to feel severe pain in my feet when walking, for inexplicable reasons. This went so far that I avoided walking whenever possible.

My job interview was successful and I became part of a small team of just ten employees at the time, including the management. In addition, I received a pair of Barefoot shoes immediately after my interview. I resolved to wear only these barefoot shoes from then on in order to alleviate my foot pain. And this really worked; after a few weeks the pain had completely disappeared.

My work was defined by the fact that we could no longer keep up with the demand. These barefoot shoes were selling almost by themselves, and as much as this was a joy, we were constantly overwhelmed with the workload. There were no direct lines, and the central phone number rang at all phones at the same time. No one had time to answer calls, and yet it had to be done. Some companies would certainly wish for such problems.

In this company, I noticed right from the start that I was surrounded by very special colleagues. The inspiring togetherness reminded me of my time at the ashram, as if we had arranged to meet here by soul contract. The Barefoot products were and still are unique and, as the unbroken demand showed, they brought real added value to the customers. It was not just an item that could have been obtained from any number of other manufacturers. In addition, almost all manufacturing steps were carried out in Germany. The management lived its vision, and that included setting up its own production, with a small team with no experience in such matters. A newly hired 26-year-old fashion designer was spontaneously given the task of setting up her own sewing shop and sewing production, and finally also the implementation of a very expensive soling machine that had yet to be built. I was put by her side and, together with her, experienced the most moving and exciting time of my entire working life. Especially my colleague's irrepressible optimism literally swept me along into almost unimaginable entrepreneurial adventures. Within the following three years, the small sales company with ten employees became a manufacturing business with more than 270 employees, including a fully established sewing shop and finally an operational soling machine. My colleague developed the new shoe models, she found cooperation partners in Germany who helped us with production technology, and she led the start-up of the soling machine, which also came from a German manufacturer. For months, we repeatedly spent entire days in the rented production hall and accompanied the arduous process of getting this first machine ready for the very special soling process. It was a very instructive time for me.

We had to find ways to optimize the organization of production planning, purchasing, and the supply of the already more than 70 sales branches. We hired new employees almost every week, and our areas of responsibility changed just as quickly. Thanks to my knowledge of the English language, I was involved in setting up and looking after the export business, and in this way, I got to know many special people all over the world.

It was a time full of inspiration and dynamics, but also full of painful experiences, especially towards the end of my employment. For many of us from the early days, our employment ended in unpleasant circumstances, caused by the burden that the unbridled growth of the company placed on management and employees. On the one hand, these years were very moving and inspiring for me, on the other hand, they were also very exhausting due to the extremely high workload and the subsequent difficult experiences.

My wife found it difficult, too, to settle back into an office job that was characterized by ever-increasing digitalization and the almost fanatical attempt to optimize every step of the employees' work in order to reduce staff or increase the workload of individual employees. After such a long time without computer and office work, the gap that had opened was difficult to fill.

The further we moved away from the end of the Mayan calendar, the more dysfunctional the world felt to us. I found it increasingly difficult to find a positive outlook on the future.

New voyages and new books

In these years, we made several vacation trips to North America during which I found, as if by chance, books that provided me with further information and made new aspects accessible to me, which were not yet known to me in this form. I would like to highlight the book *Under an Ionized Sky* by Elana Freeland. Elana shows in a frightening way how a complete military control over the earth's biosphere is achieved by means of elements introduced into the atmosphere, be it via the almost publicly known chem-trails, but also via other ingredients that create a conductivity of the atmosphere. Many HAARP facilities around the world use these chemicals to create and direct weather events. These include hurricanes, droughts, flooding from extreme precipitation, *etc.* There is a monitoring and influencing of all aspects of our lives and a control of our consciousness far beyond our imagination.

Moreover, I encountered in this time the book *Gray Aliens and the Harvesting of Souls* by Nigel Kerner, as well as the book *Reign of the Anunnaki* by Jan Erik Sigdell, which I already mentioned above.

PART 1

Nigel Kerner has dedicated himself to the subject of alien abductions and includes his more than twenty years of research in this field into his book. In his work, he met so many people to whom such an abduction had happened, that it became clear to him that these could not be only invented stories. He shows how since biblical times extraterrestrials have interfered with the genetics of humans.

According to my understanding, this happens in order to completely lock up the divine sparks of people in the physicality. All connections with which we can get into touch with our higher self and our supra-sensory abilities and perceptions are suppressed. Meanwhile, it has also been achieved by this that people cannot return freely to their origin after their physical demise, but end up in a kind of soul recycling station in the 4th dimension, from where, following the supposed karmic laws, they are immediately sent back to the earth into their next incarnation. Due to the manipulated physicality, people get entangled in ever more karmic constructs and are thus caught in an endless cycle of reincarnations. And this despite the fact that the major religions do not even recognize this concept, and the majority of people assume they are having a one-time, random existence in life.

Jan Erik Sigdell's book greatly expands the understanding on this subject. He shows how extraterrestrials have brought all of humanity under their control, and that they control all events and social life on Earth through politics, religions, and secret societies. They feed on the energies that are emitted by negative and low-vibrational emotions of the people (see also a field report later in the book that was given to me recently). The traditional religions established by the Anunnaki (extraterrestrials) are also used for this purpose. The true Jesus Christ brought us the Gnostic teachings as a way out of this, but these were very quickly replaced by the teachings of the organized Christian churches. Sigdell shows how Christ was replaced by a second, artificial Christ by means of Pauline Christianity, which again served only the purposes of the original creators of the religions.

In the further course of this book, I will give personal examples to these theses, and show how urgent it is today to leave the entire thought prison, to step into one's own divine power, and to let the light of truth shine into this world, i.e., how imperative it is to awaken now.

After completing the German edition of this book, I read the new book by David Icke, *The Trap*. I can only recommend reading it in relation to the above-mentioned titles. David elaborates extensively about the way humanities souls are being manipulated and managed from incarnation to incarnation.

When one door closes . . .

Towards the end of my work for the Barefoot Shoe Company, the psychological pressure I was feeling became ever greater.

It was certainly no coincidence that on one of the most difficult days before the end of my employment with this company, the human resources manager of the pharmaceutical company I had worked for until 1999 contacted me about a vacant position there. Since I already had great concerns about the future of my current employment, I immediately applied for this vacant position. Despite everything, I was attached to the barefoot shoe company with heart and soul. I liked my work, my colleagues, and our products. I saw a purpose in my work, and I felt that I was making a positive difference in the world. In many ways, the loss of all that together with the loss of my function and the end of my employment there was almost traumatic for me.

It took some time before I was invited to an interview for the vacant position with my first employer. During this time, I got to know the employment insurance office and the situation of an unemployed person. However, I was treated very kindly there, also because it was assumed that I would certainly be successful with the application that I had already made. In this respect, I was spared an application marathon for the time being, and unemployment benefits were approved for 18 months without any problems. This meant great reassurance for me, because financially there would be no emergency for us.

After my interview date, more time passed until mid-September before I was accepted for the new position as financial controller. Thus, after one month of unemployment, I would start work in my new position on October 1, 2017.

It was a nerve-wracking time for me because, similar to 2014, I received no response to all the other applications I had sent out simultaneously, at best a rejection.

It was clear to me at the beginning of my job that I had sold myself very well in the interview. I had not worked in Controlling for 18 years, and my predecessor was very well versed in IT matters. I understood next to nothing about what he had implemented there, and I could not build on his work.

In addition, almost from day one, some colleagues worked against me and discredited me with my supervisor and even with the advisory board. This was aggravated by my fears and insecurities which I had to cover up constantly, and by the need to present good results quickly in order to counteract the discrediting.

My employer was operating in an increasingly difficult economic environment, which was becoming more and more complicated to navigate, especially for medium-sized pharmaceutical companies. In a rapidly changing market, serious decisions had to be made on an ongoing basis. The workforce had already been significantly reduced and entire production lines had to be shut down. The constantly growing legal requirements for the production and distribution of pharmaceuticals consumed large amounts of funds that were no longer available for other relevant areas.

Even with a high level of computer affinity, I could not have counteracted these difficult circumstances so easily. The pressure exerted on the management by the above-described situation was enormous, and the legal requirement's significant impact on the available financial resources restricted the room for manoeuvre of everyone involved beyond any tolerable level. The expectations of me and my work were accordingly very high.

The trip to the Red Rocks

One bright spot in these years was our 2018 vacation trip to Arizona. I came up with this destination after a colleague showed me a photo she had taken in Sedona, Arizona. The photo appealed to me so much that I suggested a trip there to my wife.

We began planning the vacation, and over time it evolved

into a round trip through all of Arizona. It was to be one of the most beautiful trips we ever took together. And little did we know at the time that it would also be the last fulfilling vacation for a long time. In 2019, I already felt a restlessness and discord that I could not pin down to anything specific, except that a beneficial relationship with our respective employers got increasingly lost. In other ways, too, life no longer felt harmonious.

Arizona, however, was a journey into another world. We spent the first few days in Phoenix before driving on to Sedona.

Although the energetically high-vibrating area around Sedona has fallen victim to a superficial esoteric commerce, we could experience many fulfilling moments in indescribably beautiful nature settings during our stay there in the Red Rocks.

On one of these days, we had planned a hike to a vortex point in Sedona. The sky was bright blue, not a cloud in sight. With some effort, we found the starting point of our hike to Cathedral Rock. It became a hike through a fairy tale landscape with small trees, lizards, solitary birds, and we were in communion with the energies of the place. Despite the beautiful weather, we encountered other people only once, otherwise we remained alone with the sacred energy of the area and felt filled with peace.

Here, as before on our travels to special places, *e.g.*, the volcano Haleakala on the island of Maui, I had the feeling that we absorbed different energies like pieces of a puzzle, which we could not have brought into this present incarnation with this kind of diversity. Every journey, every place, and many interpersonal encounters added something to the total force and energy forming within us. And in all these places, we performed the invocation of the divine light, put the places and beings there in this light, and connected them with all the other places where we had already performed this ritual.

During our days in Sedona, we also made a trip to the Grand Canyon and explored the surroundings of this iconic natural wonder.

We went on to the town of Page in the very north of Arizona.

There we took part in an excursion into a so-called slot canyon, based on the recommendation of the local tourist information. The Antelope Canyon is better known here, but it is so crowded that you can hardly find a moment to yourself in it. So, we drove to the recommended slot canyon through the sandy desert with a Navajo tribesman on a converted pickup truck with seats on the truck bed. The ride was adventurous, and to me it felt like a roller coaster ride, only without the tracks.

We were also shown replicas of the original Navajo dwellings on the site, and finally our group of 12 was invited to explore the slot canyon. These canyons have been washed ever deeper into the ground during heavy rains, with the water then roaring through the canyon at speeds in excess of 80 mph. If there is even a slight chance of rain forecast, such tours cannot take place.

This place also had a very different aura and atmosphere and could not be compared to anything I had seen before. The play of colors in the walls of the canyon is breathtaking in the truest sense.

At this point, we were already overflowing with impressions and sensations that we could hardly process. Nevertheless, we continued the next morning. In the early dawn we found ourselves at the marina of Page, where we boarded a ship for the trip to the Rainbow Bridge in the state of Utah. It was a crisp morning and on the outside deck we had to wrap up heavily to stay warm. It took over 2 hours to cross the expanse of Lake Powell between rock massifs. The rocks lining the shore were a good indication of how high the water used to be here, the water level was now certainly more than 9 ft. below its once normal level. The approach to the landing dock led through huge rock walls standing close together, and the landscape began to remind me more and more of scenes from the Lord of the Rings.

From the dock, it took another hour of walking through a gorge of such grandiose proportions that I could imagine what it must feel like at the bottom of the Grand Canyon. It looked like a fantasy movie set on another planet. New spectacular views opened after every bend. Finally, the Rainbow Bridge was slowly coming into view. It is a huge natural stone arch that swings over a 200 ft.-wide gorge. This place is sacred to

AWAKENING

the Native Americans and exudes a very special atmosphere. We were only able to walk around the stone bridge, not under it, which is not permitted by the indigenous tribes. As soon as we reached the other side of the bridge, we were asked to go back, with the friendly hint that the captain of the ship would not wait for late participants of the trip. Thus, we had only a few minutes there, which we deeply savored.

With the completion of this trip, our stay in Page was already coming to an end, filled with an unimaginable number of impressions.

After breakfast the next morning, we started on the long leg to Chinle, AZ, where we wanted to visit the Canyon de Chelly. No sooner had we set off on our journey than large, colorful hot air balloons were rising all around us and in front of us. Against the background of the spectacular scenery of Page, this became another unforgettable sight. We got out of the car and witnessed the launch of the numerous balloons. The sight of them still accompanied us for part of the way. On our trip to Chinle, we made a detour to Monument Valley, but only looked at it from a distance because there was still a long way to go.

The sky became cloudy as we drove on, and the landscape began to look very lonely and desolate. After we arrived in Chinle, a strong wind blew gray dust across the streets, and it felt very different here than on our previous journey through Arizona. Tourism was almost non-existent in Chinle, at least at this time of year, and only a few restaurants were open. Most of the people living there are indigenous, and we probably stuck out among them.

Our hotel gave the impression that it had already closed for the winter. Chinle is located 5,600 feet above sea level, and there is regular frost and snow in winter.

The next morning, all the clouds were gone and a beautiful sunny day dawned. Our hotel was located just a short distance from the entrance to the area of the canyon. Poplar trees with bright yellow foliage were everywhere, contrasting beautifully with the bright blue sky. We drove along the rim of Canyon de Chelly, stopping frequently at viewpoints and plateaus. Time and again, spectacular views opened into this unusual landscape. We looked down into a canyon between 600 and 1,600 ft wide, with irregular but almost vertical walls on both sides. At the bottom the canyon was flat, with some smaller rock formations rising up, and in many places the same trees with the autumnal yellow leaves we had seen on the way here were growing. We were all to ourselves and surrendered to the touching impressions. At one point, we discovered a narrow rock formation pointing towards us, with petrified faces clearly visible on its front.

At the end of the canyon, we came to Spider Rock which we had already read about before our trip. Out of a wide and open area from the bottom of the canyon, this Spider Rock rises as a huge rock column with a height of more than 700 ft. This place has a special spiritual meaning according to the native peoples living there, because on this rock the Spider Woman resides, who is very important in the mythology of the Navajo and who is supposed to have taught the women how to spin cloth.

Canyon de Chelly enchanted us with its beauty. Along the opposite cliffs, we could see a multitude of ancient dwellings built into the rocks by the former inhabitants.

We spent one more night in Chinle before starting on the longest leg of our tour through Arizona. Our first destination of the day was the Petrified Forest and Painted Desert National Park. Again, we encountered a landscape that was very different from all the previous ones. Painted Desert consists of multicolored soils, and unique rounded rock formations. The landscape reminded me once again of an alien planet. There were hardly any plants to be seen, but vast whimsical-looking stretches of land that made it difficult to perceive its proportions on a comprehensible internal scale. Everything blurred into a total work of art, as if created by giants who had let their creativity run free. In the Petrified Forest, partly broken tree trunks lay around which, according to the national park's information, were petrified and looked like semi-precious stones on the inside. In the meantime, I found other explanations for this which say that these are the remains of giant trees which actually consisted of semi-precious stones. Likewise, I later learned that the landscape structure of Canyon de Chelly is understood to be a formation created by mining activities, not by erosion through a river.

At the end of our journey, we spent three more nights in Phoenix before heading back to Germany.

The attempt to destroy a society and a way out : A dream

During the *Rauhnaechte* of the Christmas season 2020 (the twelve nights between December 24 and January 6), I dreamed that next April my colleague would come into my office, very upset, in order to inform me that she had heard that they wanted to lay me off. Not already to June 30, however, but to September 30, 2021. I knew from my dream training that such dreams in the Twelve Nights of Christmas sometimes make a prediction for the corresponding month of the following year (i.e., the first Rauhnacht for January, *etc.*). I suppressed this dream and did not tell my wife about it. A little later, however, this dream would become very significant again.

From January 2020 onwards, an agenda began suddenly to dominate the world which irrevocably and permanently changed the course of all our lives. Virtually out of nowhere, the narrative of a mortal threat was brought into being and accepted as real by most of the people. At my work, this meant that we only "met" for meetings via digital conference, which took place ever more frequently and took up ever more time. On the way to the washroom or to another office, masks had to be worn, behind which the faces of colleagues were barely visible.

After the restaurants had already registered every visitor by name at the beginning of the measures, and in some cases had separated the tables with plexiglass installations, they then even had to close for months. Except for grocery stores and drugstores, customers had to register in advance for a shopping appointment, and later they could only do so with a prior PCR test and registration. Even in the sprawling outdoor areas of botanical gardens, people were no longer allowed to walk around without a mask.

Every day, the media spread new fear-mongering news about further "dangers" and restrictions and planned compulsory vaccinations. Most employers required their employees to undergo constant body injuries by means of mandatory PCR tests, even though the validity of these tests was increasingly in doubt. Almost every day, the regulations changed arbitrarily, and it was no longer comprehensible what was allowed and what not.

My wife and I began to look for a way out of this, but it was hard to find one because this agenda was being pursued in lockstep all over the world. Finally, we discovered a budding community in Paraguay. Until then, I did not really know where Paraguay was. South America, yes, but that was all I could think of. We were inspired by many YouTube videos about this community. We were especially attracted by the fact that the spiritual ideas and visions that we had worked on so intensely in the previous 25 years were being brought to life there.

And then came true what my dream from the Twelve Nights of Christmas had predicted. The managing director came to my office and told me in a few short words that my position would be eliminated in the future, and that he would therefore have to dismiss me. I was to settle everything else with the HR manager.

Even though I was treated financially in a fair way during this elimination of my position, this incident hit me very hard.

At that time, however, we had already decided to emigrate to Paraguay, because under the circumstances that now permeated all aspects of life, we could not and would not have wanted to continue living in Germany.

And in retrospect, it turned out that it was only because of the generous severance package that my resignation had brought me, that we were financially able at all to get through the time until today, when I am writing this book. Also, the timing of the termination was very good, because a short time later I would have had to give notice myself for the emigration to Paraguay, and thus would not have received any severance pay.

I was immediately released from work, and so we were able to start dissolving our home. This meant that for the 5th time in our life together, we had to give away almost all our possessions, because we could not have afforded to transport furniture and larger items to Paraguay in a container. Thus, we donated 80% of our clothing and other household appliances and equipment.

Until the very end, we were busy completing everything and only finished at the last minute. Therefore, we could not tell our families about our plans, because we literally had no time for farewell visits. We got into a cab, took the train to the airport, flew to Madrid and on to Asuncion, the capital of Paraguay. From there, we continued by minibus for 4 hours into the interior of the country and on to the community, into a tiny apartment. Here we had to start all over again, in an unfamiliar country with an extreme climate and a barren, harsh landscape. I felt driven out of my home and my life, into circumstances I would never have voluntarily entered without the unacceptable arbitrariness of the German authorities, and stranded in a country to which I would not have traveled of my own accord. One week after arriving, I had a mental breakdown and felt that I had arrived at the end of all roads.

People, trails, and adventures in Paraguay

In Germany, I had been following the regular meetings of the *Stiftung Corona-Ausschuss* (Corona Investigative Committee) since July 2020 and had also done a lot of my own research on the Corona narrative before that. I was truly convinced that one only had to explain the facts regarding this large-scale deception to the people, and then the spook would be over. More and more experts and scientists explained that here a situation was staged with forged evidence, which had no relation to reality. I also assumed that in court, such evidence should lead to an immediate conviction of the executors of this agenda. I myself attempted to educate people wherever possible, I even joined the political party *Die Basis* for a short time. In February 2021, I gave up hope in this regard. Most people blindly followed the script set by politicians, "science," and mainstream media.

In Paraguay, in the community that had taken us in, I now met many people from all walks of life who thought like me, who saw through this agenda, and wanted to protect themselves and their families against the measures and the resulting threats. It was good to finally meet only those who understood what was going on, and who were willing to face such far-reaching consequences because of this.

I was, however, not at all prepared to deal appropriately with the circumstances we encountered on site, and very quickly I was completely overwhelmed by them. The contrast to life in Germany at that time was enormous, and a pioneering spirit was demanded of the new settlers that I could not live up to.

The founders of the settlement had cultivated a large wide area, on which the development work for the building of houses had been carried out with great effort. An area and property which was completely uninhabited had been selected, in order to work freely and uninfluenced on the building of a community which would be free from the centrally controlled structures of the rest of the world. Accordingly, an entirely new world had to be created there from scratch, including roads, electricity, water, and Internet supply, solely through the power of the vision of the founders and the first settlers. All this in a very poor country in which the general standard of living is not very high, and in which there is no support for such a project from governmental institutions and authorities. It was also a huge challenge to find the appropriate professional and technical support to realize such a large-scale undertaking.

In addition, there were the tasks of developing cultivable land in order to be able to feed the emerging community as self-sufficiently as possible, to establish a school and a kindergarten, to build up a health care system, to enable the supply with items of everyday necessities via an own retail store, to create meeting places, *etc.* In short, an independent parallel world was built here which was to develop into a prototype for the liberation of mankind from the dictates of the earth-dominating powers.

Thus, we came into an environment in which two things quickly became obvious: you either had the appropriate financial means in order to be able to afford the building of your own home and to be able to support yourself with everything necessary, or elsewise you had such a huge pioneering spirit that you could build your own existence here using your own strength, and with much ingenious commitment.

These circumstances quickly and completely overwhelmed me. I was so emotionally battered by the above-described stressful experiences in Germany and the way in which the energetic key moments in 2011 and 2012 had developed, that I had to realize I would not be able to meet the requirements here.

Now we were sitting somewhere in Paraguay, had dissolved our entire household, had only modest financial means, and had to realize that we would not be able to become part of this community by our own efforts either.

And what now? Where to go now?

First, we had yet to receive our 22 boxes of personal belongings, and we had to obtain the immigration permit to Paraguay which we had already paid for, so that we could stay here legally for more than 3 months.

At that time, the rivers in South America had a very low water level, which meant that shipments from Germany took a long time to arrive. Thus, our boxes arrived in Paraguay only at the end of August.

In addition, obtaining our residence permit turned into a real drama because the various documents that were required for this from Germany took many months for the different necessary certifications, and in Germany, we had to send them back and forth several times because they were processed by two Paraguayan consulates at different locations.

To be on the safe side, we got 2 sets of documents going (certificates of birth, marriage, and good conduct). The validity of the individual documents was 3 months after issuance, and after the first completed set was lost on the express route to Paraguay, we had to put our hope on the second set which finally arrived in Paraguay in July, with only one week remaining of the certificate's validity. This set was accidentally handed over to a stranger at the delivery location and initially disappeared. With only 5 days of validity left, it finally arrived, and a trip to the immigration authorities in Asuncion could be organized for the last day of validity. This was a nerve-racking nail-biter.

We had no idea what to do now.

At least we had the opportunity to work on some projects within the community. These included the implementation of a school, the establishment of a settlers' garden to get familiar with the subject of self-cultivation, and the initial support of the newly arriving settlers. In this way, we were able to establish many new connections to people and to earn a little extra money to cover part of our costs of living.

It became a challenging personal experience for us. We also found it quite difficult to adjust to the climate in Paraguay.

Back to the north : to Mexico

During the months on site, it became clear to us, as described above, that we would not be able to afford to live permanently in this community and to build a house there. The cost would be too high, and the opportunities to earn some money too sparse, considering our range of experience. With a heavy heart, we moved on in February 2022, this time to Mexico, where in the meantime some opportunities had arisen — or so we thought.

In the area of Playa del Carmen, we had found a point of contact that supported us in obtaining a residence permit for Mexico. We traveled there in a small group of 5 people with the goal of finding a suitable place for us to dedicate ourselves to self-sufficiency, and to finding new ways for a livable future. These were noble goals but unfortunately, after only a few days in Mexico, trouble was brewing between some of us, and after only three weeks it became apparent that we would not be able to continue on this path together.

After it had been a very big and cost-intensive start to come to Mexico at all, my disappointment about this was tremendous. In order to implement the plans that were originally made in our group of five, my wife and I now would have to travel through Mexico on our own, and this challenge seemed too much. However, we had rented the place in Playa del Carmen for a couple of months and so there was time to think things through. We also took the opportunity to visit the archaeological site of Chichen Itza with its great step pyramid in the center, which Carl Calleman had used for his explanation of the waves of creation in the Mayan calendar.

A friend from Canada pointed out to me that a therapist and student of Dolores Cannon had her office south of Mexico City. This therapist is from Algeria and grew up in Germany. I contacted her and received an appointment for a regression at the beginning of April, wherein I was supposed to contribute with several personal questions and topics. With a friend from our group, I flew to Mexico City the day before the appointment, and from there we drove to Tepoztlan in a rental car.

My appointment lasted seven hours and, like other participants of such sessions with Dolores Cannon, I was taken through a series of past existences which was supposed to help me to better understand my purpose and the circumstances in this life. It turned out that in my few earthly existences, I could only to a very limited extent gain experiences regarding the way of living in this realm. Therefore, during spiritual existences in higher dimensions, I had to prepare myself relatively quickly for my time on earth.

During the regression, the question came up twice whether it was already too late for the fulfillment of my present task. This was denied; however, it was also made clear that there is no more time to waste and that I must now fulfill my purpose here. I am currently working on creating the conditions for this. And I was also told to write this book, especially, but not exclusively, for the people in my home country of Germany.

And another topic arose in Mexico parallel to the trip to Tepoztlan. My friend who accompanied me there had shortly before come across Peter Fitzek and his *Königreich Deutschland*. Almost at the same time, I had also received a hint about this "Kingdom" from an acquaintance from Germany. Thus, even before our trip to Tepoztlan, we had begun to investigate in detail about the work and ideas of Peter Fitzek, and the deeper we went into it, the more we felt drawn to the endeavors and ideas that Peter would like to live and realize, and which he has already implemented to a large extent. Together, we watched many lectures and videos by him, and on the trip to Tepoztlan, we discussed his ideas extensively.

After our return, we spent another two weeks together in the small group of five before we parted ways, at least for the time being. With two members of the group, we will probably not be able to get together again, but our friend has returned to Germany and is now already a member of the core community of the *Königreich Deutschland*. I mention this because I find it encouraging that in Germany, people are coming together and are standing up for a new and just society and for a life worth living, while respecting the non-negotiable freedoms of everyone. Of course, attempts are being made at all levels to denounce this project. Thus, it helps to research for yourself in regards to this project and then to make up your own mind.

After the others from our group had gone their separate ways, my wife and I moved into a smaller apartment for 4 more weeks in order to find back to ourselves and to be clear about our further steps. I used that time to occupy myself with the topic of brainwave synchronization ("Gateway Experience"), which was recommended to me during my regression, and every day I practiced yoga to restore my inner balance at least partially, since I had lost more and more my will to live during the past months. This had to be counteracted.

During these weeks, we sometimes met with a small English-speaking group to discuss spiritual topics. One of the participants talked about an experience he had during a shamanic journey in South America. This participant was only 26-years-old, and shortly after starting college he realized that this was no longer the right way for him and he stopped his studies overnight. He then visited indigenous peoples in Africa and South America. I would like to include his report about the mentioned shamanic journey here, because what he experienced coincides with information that I have already encountered in earlier years and which I have described earlier in the book.

I reproduce his report here as best I can:

After the ritual began, I found myself in the presence of beings which were not of the human family. These beings asked me to transfer my being over to them and to become one of them.

I made it clear to them that I would not do this.

However, further into the ritual I could observe how these beings "harvested" and transported away the emanations emitted through negative emotions and life energies of the people. I followed the flow of these energies and came to the border of our earthly plane of existence, where the extraterrestrial beings transferred these energies with a kind of funnel into their own plane of existence.

The report of this participant confirmed a lot of information on this subject I had already discovered before, e.g., that especially our negative emotions like greed, fear, anger, sadness, suffering, aggression, pain *etc.* serve as nutrient for certain beings.

During the last weeks in Mexico, I was as well made aware of the work of Dr. Joe Dispenza. I received course materials on "The Formula" and obtained his book *Becoming Supernatural*. Dr. Joe says that many people spend 70% of their time staying in negative emotions, and this statement predates the Corona narrative. During the media coverage of the Corona phenomenon, fearful emotions reached unimaginable proportions in the general population. And this fear was accompanied at the same time by a feeling of powerlessness that now unites people in passivity at a very low vibrational level. At the same time, those who can think critically and stand up for their freedoms are met with anger, rage, and the accusation that their behavior is causing the death of other people. In other words, the energetic emanations associated with negative emotions are more and more on the rise, and are now also being fueled by the fear of war and dramatic supply shortages.

Back to the south : to Paraguay

In the second half of May, we finally traveled back to Paraguay and arrived in Encarnacion on May 26, 2022. Here I am now, sitting on a wobbly stool at a tiny desk, writing this book in our small room which is located on one of the busiest streets in town. And this is where the first part of the book is slowly coming to an end. For many years, every once in a while, I thought that I would have to write a book about my life's journey because it seemed so uncommon to me. However, after the world went on its way apparently unchanged in the years 2011 and 2012, I asked myself what sense such a book would make. Even today, I sometimes ask myself who really would be interested in the path I have taken through life until now.

To you who have read this far, I express my sincere gratitude. Thank you for purchasing this book and thank you for partaking in my life's story.

First and foremost, my intention in telling this first part of the book was to show as openly and completely as possible the influences and experiences I have encountered, and the information on which my inferences and conclusions are based. In addition, however, there is a driving force that has accompanied me through the past decades, a constant feeling and awareness of a great urgency, a restlessness that will only find peace when we have let in the light of truth into this plane of being in every form; when we remember our origin and our inner wealth again in every way. And when we all together recognize irrevocably who has created the mental prison in which we currently reside, and what extensive dimensions this prison has. This is what the second part of this book will be about.

I would like to add a few words about me personally at the end of Part 1.

My life so far has been characterized by a below-average self-esteem. I have always felt inferior to other people, and I would have preferred to retreat to quiet places, such as Canada, with many books to reflect there all by myself on the meaning of existence.

I was plagued by constant fears of losing my job, of rejection, of money problems, of losses, and above all, of not having a safe place to retreat to. And I have been lacking such a place for over a year now. I am learning to deal with it, but I also know that it cannot go on like this for much longer. In this respect, it is also clear to me that I now must do my part to let the light and the love, which represent the primal ground of our being, flow from the vastness of the universe into our plane of existence.

It has also become clear to me that my contribution cannot be one that most people could do better in their own way than I could. And I realized that my soul family has now led me here to focus on the contribution I can make. This book is part of that, but so is helping to build communities that live together the alchemical process of awakening. And here begins the second part of this book.

PART 2

DEVELOPING AWARENESS

Introduction

In Part 1, I reminisced my path until today. In doing so, I certainly missed impressions, moments, and inspirations which should also have been given a place there.

Now in Part 2, it is important to me to put into words the many experiences, conclusions, and insights that have formed in me during this time, words that are more than just a superficial text.

Nowadays, there are not only countless books on spiritual topics, interpretations, and conclusions about the current circumstances and what has led to them, advice, and outlooks where it all leads to and what deeper reason everything has, but there is also provided the opportunity to deal with these topics around the clock via YouTube and Telegram channels. And many do just that. Thus, there is hardly any time for another book, and if there is, it is read over once, interrupted by the ever-flowing stream of digital information, and the content of the book soon disappears into the fog of oblivion.

In my opinion, this effect is part of a deliberate process, the part that ensures that we never dwell too long on certain thoughts, and that we are constantly flooded with distracting information from the outside.

What I also notice is that the information we receive is in many cases neutralized again, or at least questioned, by other information. These different views prevent us from focusing our attention and our creative power on a specific goal, and from arriving at our own truth and reality. We are mostly trapped somewhere out there in digital worlds, in videos, posts, and discussions that others are leading.

But the truth is within us. And only with our very own truth and our whole focus on it, we can use our creative power purposefully for our liberation. That is what this is all about now. And this book shall be your companion until you have found your truth and create out of this truth light, liberation, and awakening into your divine being and share this experience with as many people as possible, so that together we become and are the light that can show the inhabitants of the earth the way home.

I believe this can only happen on the level of the incarnated souls; it cannot be accomplished from the outside. That is why we had to come to earth, and if you have read on until here, then you belong to those who have made it their life's mission to serve the people NOW as a guide into the light and into freedom.

The solution lies within

At the beginning of this second part, I would like to tell a story that has led me, among other things, to the conviction that to find the way for ascending into the light in this realm of being, is indeed only possible through incarnated human beings.

To explain this, I will go far back to the year 1980. At that time, I lived with my family in Freiburg/Breisgau and, as during my entire school time, I read a lot of books. In a bookstore, I came across a new book series by the author Stephen R. Donaldson. At that time, I certainly would not have guessed that his work would accompany me for another 3½ decades, because that is how long it took the author to write the final volume of the series, entitled *The Last Dark*.

The book series tells the story of Thomas Covenant who suddenly finds himself in a parallel world. I will briefly summarize the contents here:

Thomas Covenant lived in the USA, and there he fell ill with leprosy. Nobody was able to say how this could have been possible. After a long therapy which led to a stabilization of his health, he could return home. By then, however, he had lost some of his fingers and the sense of touch and feeling in his arms and legs, hands, and feet.

By now, word of his illness had spread and pretty much everyone around him no longer wanted to have anything to do with him. He was considered a leper, but people did not want to express this directly to him. The residents of his village agreed that they would take care of any necessary errands for him in such a way that he would no longer have to come to the village himself. He only had to tell them what he needed, and they would take care of it for him.

For Thomas Covenant, it was a psychologically difficult,

even traumatic existence. His wife also soon left him so that he ended up living completely alone. Unwilling to be isolated in this way, he went out into the village from time to time to run his own errands.

During one of these outings, he was hit by a vehicle and subsequently hospitalized, being in an unconscious state, in a kind of coma. He himself, however, found himself in a parallel world that felt real to him in every way. And there he stayed for months, while his worldly body, still in a coma, stayed in the hospital for only a few days. In this parallel world, he was regarded as a savior and re-embodiment of a past hero. However, it was almost impossible for him to succumb to these circumstances, and when the feeling in his hands, arms, legs, and feet also returned as a result of treatment with healing clay spread on his limbs, he found himself mentally at the limits of his endurance.

As the narrative progresses, it becomes obvious to the reader that the world in which Thomas Covenant found himself was ruled by a Lord Foul. There, beyond the arc of time, he had subjugated all creation to his interests and appropriated the corresponding powers, which ultimately aimed at eluding the limits set by the Creator of the world. Thereby, he subjected all habitats to his dictates, and in the end, the destruction of the whole world was supposed to occur.

The Creator knew about all this. However, an intervention of his own was not possible for him because then he would destroy the arc of time and with it his own creation, together with all the beings in it. For a long time, he searched for a human being who had the mental condition to be able to defeat Lord Foul and thus to save creation. Thereby the Creator had to trust completely that Thomas Covenant, whom he deemed suitable for this task, would find a way to realize this task all by himself. Thomas was also called "The Unbeliever" because he could not believe in the reality of the parallel world. His wedding ring of white gold, which he had continued to wear despite the separation from his wife, contained a special power through which Thomas was enabled to perform supra-sensory actions and healings by aligning his consciousness and his thoughts. His capability to defeat Lord Foul also depended on the appropriate use of his ring. Thomas was not aware of this but Lord Foul was, and so he had to do everything possible to possess this ring himself.

Up to the 6th volume (1983), I read this story while still being a student in high school. The plot was always characterized by the fact that Thomas Covenant, after each return to his earthly life, was again transferred to the parallel world by certain circumstances. Time there jumped forward by decades, while for him only weeks, at the most months had passed. And at no time did he get any instructions or hints from the Creator of the world which would have helped him to understand what had happened to him and what he had been chosen for.

What always stayed with me from this story is the concept that the divine creative power cannot intervene from the outside, but that redemption, liberation, and healing must come from within.

This seems also to be the case now here during our time on earth. The people with the power to liberate this plane of existence and to reconnect it with the All-Oneness of Creation, are not yet aware of this task in every consequence.

The star children, the voluntarily incarnated souls, and the light warriors each carry within themselves parts of what is needed to become whole. In order to become whole, further elements are necessary which can be found in special places and above all, through the encounter with other people. This process happens mostly unnoticed, and only when all elements are united, the awakening of these souls can happen.

This sounds like the template for a new fantasy novel, and one would like to read such a story sitting in an armchair by the fireplace in a house at the edge of the forest until the happy ending, where the universal light floods the whole world by itself, heals everything and everyone, and the soul families are reunited. We expect that others will fix it, and if not, we project the redemption of the world onto future generations and future times, and continue to live in the illusion of this reality.

Now this here is not a nice story, but it is NOW the moment when we may realize that WE are the ones who came here to open the doors into the light; we, who cannot imagine at all how we are supposed to make it happen. It is just so that no one will come along after us. Hence this book, and the call to all of you to awaken together and to become whole.

The concept of tomorrow

According to my understanding, there are forces or existences in this world level which have a consciousness but no divine spark of light of their own, as this belongs to the ensouled human being. However, these beings manage successfully to feed on the energies of suffering which people emanate regularly. And they have found ways to steer the people in such a way that these have created a reality which offers the ideal precondition to produce ever more suffering.

Nevertheless, and I have already spoken about this in the first part of the book, there has been a change in the energetics of the universe and in all its levels of being, an increase in vibration. And in this new level of vibration, the artificial construct which was created by the soulless beings will no longer be able to exist. One way or another, a higher vibrational level will permeate in such a way that the truth can no longer be concealed.

It is my understanding that the ascent of humanity and the earth into this new vibrational level is to take place during embodiment. Therefore, there can be no intervention from the outside because this would lead to a destruction of the physical existence of the earthly levels of life.

So, what is happening right now?

For a long time, the consciousness of the earth-born people has been shaped and narrowed in such a way that they no longer recognize their own divine creative powers and above all, no longer use them kindly in love and harmony. Instead, they are told from the outside how to use these creative powers. And this happens entirely unconsciously. Through the established world view and the channels of mass communication, mental images are given which only become reality through the powers of the consciousness of almost all of humanity and their correspondingly directed creative forces. Also, a system was successfully established which strips all newborns of their divine origin and signs them over to an artificial state entity as property. For more profound information about this topic,

I recommend, for example, the two books by Peter Freiherr von Liechtenstein *Freiheit durch Wahrheit* (*Freedom Through Truth*), volumes 1 and 2.*

We are currently in a kind of race towards an invisible finish line. This finish line marks the moment when the vibration around us has increased to such an extent that our low vibrating reality can no longer exist in it. You can also think of it as a dam that can hold back water, but if it cannot release pressure through drains, it will eventually break. Controlled release allows water to reach the area behind the dam without causing destruction. If that does not happen, then the dam breaks and everything behind it goes down in an enormous tidal wave.

My understanding is that the soulless entities are in the process of completing a plan that will allow them to transfer the ensouling sparks of light from humans to themselves. One of the tools for this is transhumanism. This project is being pushed forward on unimaginably many levels and with unimaginably many methods. And it is very important for the soulless entities that no awakening takes place until the completion of their project.

How can you reliably keep people from awakening? And how has it been possible to successfully keep humanity away from it until today?

This could be achieved because people in their imagination are always postponing the time of awakening into the future, and they are always leaving this awakening to future generations.

Over the past 27 years, I have noticed that there were repeatedly wise forecasts and analyses that predicted salvation and awakening within the next 3, 5, 7, 15, even 25 or more years. Every Telegram user encounters such predictions almost daily. When one of these milestones is reached, nothing happens and a new prediction has already been safely established, postponing the awakening for another few months or years into the future. And all the while, the transhumanist agenda continues. I am convinced that this "projecting everything into the future" is one of the most successful thought models of those beings that want to hijack the light force of humanity,

---

* Unfortunately, these have not yet been published in English.

and I am also aware that this statement of mine may cause resistance from those well-meaning prophets. Because in the spiritual community, there are presently only a few who are aware what they cause with this projection into the future. They are postponing the salvation of mankind far beyond the timeline by which the forces dominating mankind have envisaged their final completion of the transhumanist agenda.

It is not by chance that we all find ourselves in this situation together. The vibration of consciousness in our plane of existence has been manipulated to such an extent that we have now lost almost all touch with reality. Our thought contents are the result of a controlled programming. And the programmers have apparently foreseen all aspects and possible loopholes far in advance and fixed them accordingly.

Most people today exchange ideas within the framework and level of their respective programming, and no longer on the level of their true being.

That is why *now*. This is what we, the volunteers, star children, and light warriors came here to do during the last century. Today we awaken. For our children, for Gaia, for all other kingdoms of life on earth. And for the Universe itself.

The way into the darkness

I have encountered many tales and stories that tell how the light-filled souls arrived at their present state of being.

Mostly, it begins with the fact that consciousness parts or soul parts have split off from the divine All-Oneness in order to be able to make new experiences. If everything is always one, and everything and everyone is always aware of their complete connectedness with the All-One, then certain perceptions and experiences simply cannot be had. The state of being is always the same, and everyone knows everything and is one with it. The separation into individual entities should allow a view on the All-Oneness from the outside and thus make new experiences possible.

That may be the reason why the earth originated as an experience level. A level of experience which many ages ago still exhibited an essentially subtler and higher vibration, and on which slowly and gradually a biosphere developed into which the human souls could move in and out and become creatively active. A development took place during which these souls gradually passed from a very subtle form of existence into a lower and lower vibrating one. The capability to swing in and out of the earth plane remained for a long time though. On this level of experience, finally the advanced civilizations of the Lemurians and the Atlanteans developed, and in these times also the influence of the "soulless" beings began to make itself felt. There was an influencing on the consciousness of the human souls, and this led to an increasing separation from the idea of divine connectedness and unity towards an individual consciousness. Thence, the idea arose instead of wanting to create independently and only for oneself, without considering the effects on others.

At the time of Atlantis, for example, the powers of crystals and energy grids were used, which connected the earth plane with the forces of the primordial cosmos. In this way, the elemental forces of the universe were used for creations and manipulations on the earth plane. However, universal laws were violated, *e.g.*, in the field of genetics. What happened on the earth level took forms which would have had repercussions on the whole universe and which would have been no longer compatible with the law of creation.

Insofar, it came to the big cataclysms which led in consequence to the destruction of Atlantis, like the Lemurian civilization had probably ended before, too.

The sinking of Atlantis had also the effect that the energy grid was removed from the earth sphere, which was used in the times of Atlantis and with which it was possible for the Atlanteans to channel and use universal forces for their purposes. Thus, the creative framework for the human souls was from then on clearly restricted.

However, this did not change the fact that the divine spark of light, with which unlimited creative forces go along, is still inherent in the human being. These creative forces can however no longer be used against creation in the same way as it was possible at the time of Atlantis through the energy grid and the misuse of the crystal powers.

Nevertheless, the destructive power which was present at

that time has looked for other ways to make a renewed attempt. Nowadays, it seems that earthbound humanity has no more connection to its origin, its abilities, and its purpose of existence. We are surrounded by an artificially created "reality." This "reality" is only sustained and developed through control of the creative forces of mankind.

Time and again, we come across information that a great deal can be accomplished through the focused attention of a certain number of people who come together for a common purpose, for a common meditation, or prayer. And exactly this fact has been used to bring about the present state of human society. By means of school, university, media of all kinds, the "sciences," and the systematic elimination of the knowledge of indigenous peoples and cultures, the focus of all of humanity has been directed to an artificial reality construct which has assumed a valid reality on earth, through the acceptance and belief of the people living in it.

Under the cover of this "reality," the preparation of transhumanism and the goal of harvesting the divine sparks of light can be further advanced.

While I write these lines, I am aware that even well-disposed readers could reach the limits of their acceptance with this. My statements may sound so out of touch and inconceivable that you may want to shake your head and ask, "What has happened to Stefan, how can we bring him back down to earth?" Some people may think like this. And this is exactly the protective mechanism built into our thinking system; this is where the border lies which we have not yet crossed. Here the system protects itself, in that those who have ventured to this point of thinking, recoil to turn back into the prison construct and look for a solution there.

A self-protecting and self-preserving system we have here, well thought out, long prepared, and meeting all eventualities.

That is why right now many beings from other parts and vibrational levels of creation have incarnated here among us. Beings who can sense that a great injustice is happening here and who bring with them the ability to fully remember their origin and mission, who have a certain immunity to the mental control on this plane of existence.

And that is the reason why I am writing this book, respectively, why I was given this task during my regression. In the first place, it is addressed to these souls. And since I am to write it originally in German and for German readers, it seems to be that particularly in Germany, there are many of these special incarnations.

So, I continue to make myself available as a tool for my higher self, so that what I write in the following can fulfill the purpose of this book, and can reach the souls and the still hidden memories of its readers.

In the second place, my book is addressed to those people who feel in their hearts that something is very wrong here. You are the ones to whom the awakened light workers will come first. And you are the ones who will subsequently carry the light of love and truth into this world plane, together with the voluntarily incarnated souls.

And everyone who absorbs these lines is being prepared in the heart of their being for what is about to happen. The ability to allow these changes to take place is thus created.

In the following, let us look together at the condition of the world in these times, and in doing so bring the light of realization into the many different narratives.

"Opportunity" Corona

Why opportunity? Because what happened during the time the Corona narrative was being played out has left all boundaries of supposedly acceptable proportionality. When we have worked through this narrative, then we can dissolve the whole artificial construct of lies by which our "civilization" has been formed. And then we will rediscover beyond it our very own home base.

I already mentioned in the first part that after my return to Germany in 2012 and the experiences that my wife and I were allowed to gather, especially in our work life, I increasingly got the feeling that life and the world no longer ran in the former "harmony." The general quality of well-being had deteriorated.

At the beginning of the year 2020, there were first news

about an alleged new virus which had been discovered in China. And of course, unfortunately, a lady from China traveled to Bavaria with this very virus right at the beginning of the new narrative and passed on this virus, while having a supposedly symptom-free infection. It was later clarified that she was suffering from flu or cold symptoms, but this fact did not find its way into the mass media, because all the media outlets had already been put on course how to handle this story.

So, there were a few "infected" and hardly any symptomatic cases. With such few cases, a worldwide health emergency could not be declared immediately. The whole thing was thus only observed at first.

And then Germany again came to the forefront. Without symptomatically ill people, no health emergency would work. So, sick people had to be created, in a new and innovative way.

There was a test procedure developed by Mr. Kari Mullis for which he was honored with the Nobel Prize, and this test was made the crown witness of the "pandemic." Kari Mullis had previously commented on what his invention can and cannot do. Unfortunately, Mullis died in August 2019, a few months before his invention would be used to hold the entire world population hostage and unravel social life.

Coincidentally, some politicians and scientists had already simulated a potential Covid-19 pandemic in the second half of 2019 and considered countermeasures during this simulation.

Still in January 2020, the problem of insufficient Covid suspect cases was solved by hastily compiling a PCR test for the "novel" SARS-CoV-2 virus, using computer simulations based on the older SARS-CoV-1 virus. This test was primarily performed on symptom-free individuals. This introduced the narrative of symptom-less infected and supposedly infectious positive test subjects. Kari Mullis would certainly have had some comments on this, especially on the application of his test. If one enlarges the samples in potencies beyond 25 cycles to an almost immeasurable extent, then one finds all possible cell products (including the remnants of damaged cells as they arise, for example, through the exposure to 5G radiation), which one can then identify as the searched-for alleged virus. Until today, it has not been possible to visually detect or isolate the Corona virus. Only computer models have been built to define what must be "found" in order to proclaim that it is this virus. What actually is found are fragments or residues of dead cells that are then supposed to be evidence that there exists a covid infection. False positive testing is what this must be called. Kari Mullis and many other scientists have also repeatedly confirmed that the PCR test is unsuitable for detecting an infection, even more so in people who are absolutely symptom-free and do not develop any symptoms even after testing.

The result of these actions was that a number base was conjured up out of thin air that could be used for the narrative of a worldwide pandemic, by introducing the symptom-less infected patient and then also declaring positively tested deceased people without Covid symptoms as having died of Covid.

At this point, I must press the stop button for a moment. At this point, we all need to clearly recognize and be aware that all those involved in representing, pushing, justifying, and implementing this narrative in any way, shape, or form, share responsibility for all the consequences that this has had in the meantime.

So much of the discussion on this subject plays out on only a superficial level. It goes back and forth whether this disease exists, whether the virus came out of a laboratory, what the long-term consequences of this disease are, whether the right measures have been taken, and so on. But before any discussion makes sense, it must be checked whether there is a basis for discussion at all. And this basis does not exist until today.

Instead, "vaccines" were developed on the non-existent basis, and administered to the people.

Currently in Germany, a new heavy infection wave for the autumn of 2022 is announced. The 4th injection has already been administered, and there is talk about new "vaccinations" with improved "vaccines" in the fall. And by the way, the German government has spent over €1-billion per month on the public PCR tests, besides all the other money that has been scattered all over the world. For example, companies like Lufthansa were completely subsidized through this crisis, and even all the German's favourite European vacation destinations were fully financed by German tax money despite having no visitors (this happened through the many millions of Euros which the German government had funneled to the EU).

My concern here is not to explain in detail which money was paid where and where not. My concern is the overall picture.

To me, it became already obvious at the end of February 2020 that something was very wrong here. At that time, I followed the numbers of "infected" people in China daily for several weeks. These numbers rose relatively quickly to about 75,000, and after that it went only in slow motion to around 80,000 infected people. By the end of February, there were approximately 75 to 200 new "infections" per day in China. With a total population of 1.4 billion people, that is rather irrelevant. We are also talking here about allegedly *infected* people, not dead people. And I still remembered well the 2018 flu season, in which almost 26,000 infected people died in Germany alone, out of a population of 82 million. If one were to extrapolate these numbers to the Chinese population, one would arrive at a figure of almost 440,000 dead. This numerical example alone made it clear to me that there could be no really threatening situation here.

The point here is to recognize that a narrative was initiated worldwide at the same time and by all governments together, which could have been seen through very easily on closer inspection. With so many different countries allegedly affected, some politician or scientist should have been able to determine that there was no extreme health emergency. There were such people, but almost nowhere in the world were they officially listened to. And the entire mass media worldwide refused to discuss the matter objectively, and stood by the given narrative without resistance.

Here I would like to raise the question whether this is the first and only case in which such a concerted action was carried out against humanity?

Certainly not. More on this follows in a moment.

We are confronted today with the fact that during the years of the Corona narrative, there has been a massive redistribution of financial wealth from small and medium earners onto large earners; that permanent social and health damages have been caused, for whose care and treatment there is no infrastructure; and that the digital control of people has once again been substantially intensified after the tightening of control already carried out since 9/11. Systems have been developed that make it possible to tie people's freedom to certain conditions and to enforce this by means of digital control mechanisms and tools. For example, no access to businesses, events, transportation, *etc.* is granted without a prior PCR test or vaccination. This technology is now ready to be applied in other areas, such as "climate protection."

Before we broaden our focus from the past two years to larger periods of time, I would like to point out some further examples of the central influence on humanity and the artificial creation of narratives.

Climate

We are being told that we urgently must do something to slow down global warming.

Now even regarding this topic, in scientific papers you can find very different conclusions than those that the mainstream uses for their agenda of global warming. Ultimately, this is also a narrative used to control the population, restrict freedoms, and redistribute wealth.

Let us just leave aside the question of whether there is global warming in the form propagated, and let us instead look at the measures that are being taken to counteract it.

To begin with a personal example, in the last few years in Germany we have used standard halogen light bulbs for as long as possible, and only did without some electrical appliances such as TV set, vacuum cleaner, and automatic coffee maker. Nevertheless, the electricity provider confirmed with each annual bill that our electricity consumption was below the value for an extremely energy-efficient one-person household. We paid €26 per month for an 840-sq-ft apartment. With conventional hob, laundry machine, kettle, fridge/freezer, computer, radio appliances, cell phones, halogen bulbs, *etc.* Thus, it is possible to live a normal life without consuming excessive energy.

The government has proposed to generate energy from wind and solar power plants and to switch to electric mobility. In this regard, it is highly recommended to watch the lectures of Professor Dr. Hans-Werner Sinn on this topic. What should be clear to us, however, even without his lectures, is that our power generation capacities will never be even remotely sufficient for the conversion of individual mobility to electric drive. This means that nuclear and conventional power plants should not be shut down but should be maintained and expanded. Since this is not planned and not appropriate, it would be better to do without electromobility.

Professor Sinn also points out another circumstance. Wind and solar energies are not always fully available. There are times in which these energy sources provide almost no electricity, *e.g.*, when the sun is not shining or the wind is not blowing. In these cases, too, most of the conventional power plants would have to be kept operational in order to be able to step in during such times. This means the power plants would have to remain manned, maintained, and supplied with energy sources. But that is not intended in the German government's concept. We can already guess what really shall be achieved with this narrative: the abolition of individual mobility for most of the population.

Also, regarding this topic, we may ask ourselves which effects the extraction of the raw materials to produce lithium batteries on a large scale would have on humans and our earth. Already today, entire landscapes are permanently devastated where lithium is mined (for example, in Chile). This process would inevitably increase exponentially. The same applies to rare earths which are extracted in the Congo, for example, with the use of child labor. Most people do not think about this, nor about the exorbitant burden on the environment that would result from the mass disposal of the huge batteries.

The people which are led into this narrative by the mass media ignore all further information, buy electric bicycles and scooters, and increase the whole problem.

In this context, one should also investigate in more detail who started the movement "Fridays for Future," and where the money comes from that is used to finance this movement. The children and young people who are instrumentalized and emotionalized for this purpose, represent narratives that have been given to them. What they have not been told is what the consequences of the measures taken for "climate protection" will be. For example, how rainfall will be reduced by huge wind farms, what the psychological and ecological effects will be of a landscape where wind farms dominate the horizon instead of forests, along with the physical and vibrational effects on all living beings, especially birds and insects.

What is not talked about publicly at all are the free energies; developments and inventions that could have been introduced and made available already in the times of Nikola Tesla. For this cause, humans could take to the streets after all, for the broad availability of free energy sources for everyone and for the independence from paid for electricity. Instead of spending one billion € per month for the PCR citizen tests alone, the German government could instead have made such a system available to many.

Further examples

A similar, centrally controlled narrative can be found in the "Black Lives Matter" movement, as well as in the subject of gendering. While Germany is in a lockdown, while German police officers use unimaginable violence against their own fellow citizens on peaceful demonstrations against the Corona measurements, tens of thousands of people gather in Germany — without observing distancing rules and motivated and supported by the police with luminous displays — to demonstrate against the treatment of an American citizen by the police in the USA. Everyone should think about this for themselves whether this makes sense, and how much independent thinking still takes place in people's minds.

Again, this is not about discussing the mentioned events in every detail, but basically to show examples which make clear how mankind is steered and controlled by organized deception and misdirection.

With this, I come back to the question whether this form of manipulation is a new kind of mind- and thought-control or not.

A fake history

For this purpose, I invite you to familiarize yourself with some of Raik Garve's work together with me.

About ten months ago, I was made aware of talks that Raik Garve had done on the channel "Neue Horizonte TV." Since then, I have followed many hours of interviews and talks with Raik on this and on other channels. What was hard to comprehend at first, now seems quite conceivable to me.

Raik is a studied physician and health teacher. For a long time, he had the feeling that the history doctrine conveyed to us cannot be true, which motivated him to delve deeply into this topic. He found out that the history taught in schools and universities today is almost entirely made up. We are supposed to believe this story and thus also the explanation of who or what we supposedly are, and above all, where we supposedly come from.

During his research and study of this topic, Raik encountered scientists who had conducted similar investigations. What they found out was that from a certain point in time in the past backward, specific chronologies and historical sequences could not have taken place as they were conveyed to us. The work of the Russian researcher Anatoly Fomenko was one of Raik's main inspirations. Fomenko wrote several extensive volumes on the subject of "History: Fiction or Science?"

If we look at the past 1,000 years, Raik points out three major caesuras. In each case, the spiritual, cultural, social, and technical level of the earth inhabitants was gradually developed downwards by a concerted intervention from the outside, by means of appropriate technology which deliberately caused disasters. In the dormant periods between these large-scale events, new narratives were introduced and established. Those humans who still had a connection to the level of knowledge before the disaster were for the most part deliberately persecuted and killed. In this way, mankind could be brought to lower and lower levels of consciousness and could intentionally be made controllable by the same soulless forces which I have already described in the chapter "The way into the darkness."

The first great caesura staged by outside forces took place

approximately 1000 – 1200 A.D., in the form of a deluge which was obviously caused using correspondingly developed technology. Today, in conventional history, this is called a plague epidemic. Up to this caesura, the Tartarian high culture dominated on the earth. The so-called age of the giants, whose existence nowadays has been completely removed from the historiography, also falls into this time frame.

In the recovery phase that followed this cataclysm, new narratives were introduced, while the former Vedic-Tartaric high culture slowly began to recover.

The second major caesura occurred between 1400 and 1500 A.D. and was again brought about by a natural catastrophe, this time with a worldwide mud flood that literally depopulated the cities of that time.

This was followed by another period of recovery. The population was traumatized, and this circumstance was used purposefully to implement the organized religions even more strongly, in order to achieve a centralized spiritual control of mankind.

There were still remnants of the former Vedic-Tartaric high culture, which was finally eliminated completely between 1700 and 1800 A.D. during a global war. In addition, the years of historical events were manipulated afterwards, so that when the history books speak of 2000 years since the lifetime of Jesus Christ, it really might have been only 1000 years.

Since then, a mankind exists which is not conscious anymore of its origin and which also has no access anymore to their own divine creative power.

Above I describe the historical processes in such a way as elaborated by Raik. Personally, I am not sure whether the so-called Tartar high culture was not as well an expression of a world-dominating power, which faded away in order to make the further devolution of mankind possible. The Tartar civilization also used central and regional state control mechanisms to suppress mankind and to move it further away from its inherent creative power onto the path of devolution.

The American author Gregg Braden was told a respective story in New Mexico during an encounter with an indigenous group.

AWAKENING

After mankind had lived for a long time in complete harmony with nature, the elements, and the natural beings, in a time in which one could also speak with the stars, it came about for inexplicable reasons that people lost this connection and the memory of it. They now lived separated from nature and the natural beings and used a large part of their energy to defend themselves against these supposedly threatening forces of nature, instead of using their power harmoniously.

Through dreams, people began to recall their previous existence in harmony with nature, and they also recalled their former abilities that they had been able to use in previous times. They remembered that they had the power to heal themselves from within, and that they themselves could communicate with the elements, the celestial beings, and the stars.

Thus, people began to create things on the outside to remind them of these abilities. However, that was exhausting because each further creation in the outside demanded more strength and energy from them. Instead of bringing their inherent abilities back to life, they projected them outward. They laid cables to communicate over long distances, they developed medicine to ingest, chemistry for farming, and so on. The more they did this, the higher the price they had to pay. The end of this story is being written in these times, and its outcome is not yet certain.[†]

This story shows how the capabilities that were once inherent in earthly beings now exist only in limited and sometimes degenerated forms on the outside. Instead of using telepathy, we use cell phones, instead of cultivating plants in harmony with the elemental beings, we spray plants and soil with toxic chemicals, instead of healing ourselves from within, we treat our bodies with techniques and chemicals that mostly aggravate the problem by creating new problems, and so on.

This development was set up by the three catastrophes mentioned above. Therein could lie an explanation for the "forgetting."

Let us now have a look at the Cheops pyramid.

According to conventional history books, this structure is about 4,500 years old. Before this pyramid, there were no comparable structures that could explain how a culture could develop that could build such constructs. The Cheops pyramid signals in any form the culmination of a culture, for thereafter

---

† Recounted by the author from: Atlantis, Pyramiden & Kundalini *https://www.youtube.com/watch?v=c9G-Kl2RwjM*.

the ability to create similar structures of such quality continued to decline.

Even using the most modern construction technology, it would not be possible nowadays to build such a pyramid. The sarcophagus, for example, was carved out of a rock that could not be shaped in a similarly precise manner with the most powerful equipment today. There are drillings in the granite which were drilled faster and more thoroughly into the hard rock than this would be possible with the most powerful drills today.

There are innumerable details concerning the construction of this pyramid which could never have been mastered by a supposedly almost stone-age culture with the technological means of that time. Thus, also this narrative from the more distant history cannot be correct.

Alternatively, it is assumed that the Egyptians themselves found the Cheops pyramid at that time, hidden in the desert sand that had piled up on it. Likewise, the Sphinx cannot have been built only 4,500 years ago, because the rock from which it was built shows very strong signs of a water erosion, which could not have occurred in this intensity over just 4,500 years. In order to show such a water erosion, the Sphinx would have had to have been built at least 9,500 to 10,000 years ago, possibly even earlier.

Further examples could be listed why the classical historiography cannot be correct and must have been made up.

Again, I am not interested in discussing this in every detail. Rather, it is important to me to point out that "history" was invented, and to ask to which purpose this could have happened.

More examples

Regarding this question, I would like to include some more topics. In addition to the Corona narrative, which has already been discussed in some detail, there are the subjects of 9/11 as well as the moon landing.

With 9/11, there are many inconsistencies which we already discussed in Part 1 of this book. In the end, the destruction of the buildings has been caused by the American government itself by means of explosions and the use of other high-tech weapons. On the one hand, the wars in Iraq and Afghanistan could be justified by this event, and on the other hand, measures could be taken and enforced to prevent a spiritual awakening. The shock wave of this event alone has clearly set back the spiritual development of mankind.

That the moon landings most probably also never took place, was much more difficult for me to accept. During the (alleged) first moon landing in 1969, I lived with my family in the USA, and my father trained at that time on the same type of aircraft with which the moon landing astronauts were trained, the T-38.

I still remember the excitement among the people at that time and how I was allowed to stay up late in the evenings because there were broadcasts of the moon mission on television. A great fascination with space travel and outer space accompanied me throughout my childhood and youth. I followed the space shuttle program with fascination and I saw myself flying alone through space on a spaceship at night.

The first slight doubts came to my mind around 2010 when my boss at the time mentioned that the moon landings could not be real. He held up his small calculator and remarked that one could not fly through space and land on a foreign celestial body with such tiny computing power. Any of our office computers today would have greater computing power than the computers the Apollo space capsules carried with them.

Over the past 12 months, I have encountered this theme many times, and Raik Garve also mentions it in his listing of the "little" lies of history. Among the small lies he counts the Covid narrative, the vaccination lies (in general, vaccinations are to be considered counterproductive), the 9/11 lie, and the moon landing lie. Among the big lies he counts how our true origin was veiled and how the staged catastrophes described above were used for the subsequent manipulation of consciousness.

How does everything fit together?

In the meantime, I have thought a lot about how the work of Carl Calleman can be brought into alignment with the findings of Anatoly Fomenko and Raik Garve.

At least concerning the 6th and 7th creation wave, the different findings of the two sides cannot be reconciled. Carl derives his theories concerning these two waves of creation from the events as they were supposed to have occurred according to the conventional history books. Assuming that a large part of the historiography was simply invented to make today's world narrative possible, then Carl's derivations do not fit anymore, because the events to which he refers have presumably not taken place or, respectively, in a modified form, however, at completely different times.

Nevertheless, I consider it very probable that the "extraterrestrial" interventions into the history of mankind during the past 12,000 years were possible only because of the corresponding cosmic energies as these were made visible by the Mayan calendar.

12,000 years ago, during a great catastrophe, the advanced civilization of Atlantis is said to have perished. At this time, the building energies that would later dominate the 6th wave of creation clearly began to make themselves felt. Up to this time, a holistic consciousness with corresponding unfiltered access to the spiritual spheres (energy of the 5th creation wave, which began about 100,000 years ago) dominated in the universe and on earth. The 6th wave was characterized by the fact that the light of creation shone only on the left hemisphere of the brain, whereas the right hemisphere of the brain, which is responsible for access to the supernatural (perceptions that go beyond the 5 physical senses), was in darkness. Thus, it became possible to install the many "resets" described above, without people being able to recall afterwards what had been before. Mankind was therefore very easily programmable in this time, without an opportunity to verify the newly instilled contents. Also, the 7th creation wave with the accompanying complete darkness on both sides of the brain (see explanations to the Mayan calendar in the first part of the book) supported this circumstance still further.

In this respect, Calleman's work continues to make great sense to me, also in relation to the drama we are currently experiencing in the world. As already explained, the 9th wave of creation began in March 2011 which found its completion in October 2011 together with all other waves of creation. The universal energy thereby established shone the divine light again on both sides of consciousness, on the male and female principle equally. Thus, it became possible for people to connect again with their origin. And this potential cannot be permanently withheld from mankind. Therefore, a great effort is being made to keep it away from the awareness of humankind, at least long enough in order to complete the harvesting of the souls in terms of transhumanism. Like the reawakening of telepathic abilities at the beginning and during the 8th wave of creation was diverted to technology (among other things smartphones), so today the narrative of genderism is used to steer the harmonious inner union of the male and female principle into dysfunctional ways of expression.

In recent weeks, I have encountered more and more reports that people who have been administered mRNA "vaccines," have subsequently experienced personality changes as well as energetic changes. The sensory and thinking faculties undergo changes. Memory also seems to be affected.

My intuition tells me that by means of the administration of these preparations and the active and auxiliary substances contained in them, the ability of people to reconnect with their divine origin is to be interrupted. These efforts are supported by radio waves, genetically modified foods, and toxic substances released into the atmosphere, including nanoparticles.

It is important to me to share the above information and sources with you, so that I can now, based on that, put these developments and events into a larger context.

The real descent of mankind

I have already spoken about the fact that earthbound humanity once had been able to move freely in and out of embodiment. Even at the beginning of the incarnation cycle into a physical body, they could keep this body in a completely healthy and harmonious state by means of their spiritual power, for as long as they liked. Death in today's sense did not exist and therefore there were no "corpses." When a soul concluded that it wanted to end its current earthly incarnation, it dissolved its physical body in the divine light and returned to an ethereal state. And at that time, there was also not yet an alien-controlled receiving station in the 4th dimension from which the "deceased" souls were immediately sent back into the next earthly incarnation.

Obviously, the universal frequency levels changed in a way which made possible an existence that was ever further separated from the All-One. In this process, an increasingly more individual experience became possible for the souls during their incarnations.

This descent into ever denser and lower vibrating existences brought it with it that humans lost the reference to their own origin (see also the narration above which was transmitted to Gregg Braden).

And at this point, those entities showed up which did not have their own divine light spark, and which have therefore developed a plan over the millennia which was meant to lead to today's transhumanism.

At a certain point in time, these beings succeeded in influencing the perception of human beings in such a way that they could no longer stay in touch with the higher spheres of consciousness during incarnation, and even in "death" they were directed into a 4-dimensional intermediate plane from where their next incarnation was then initiated.

According to the traditions of indigenous peoples, for example the Hopi from Arizona, there was a series of global cataclysms up to the present time, which in each case led to an almost complete extinction of mankind. It seems to me that we are not talking here about the past 1,000 to 2,000 years of recent history, but about universal times like those of Lemuria and Atlantis. And I assume that after each of these cataclysms, the consciousness of mankind devolved into lower spheres of vibration, up to the modern times in which people are now being prepared for the final step, namely the separation of the animating light from the spirit of man by means of transhumanistic methods. And here certainly the ingredients of the so-called Covid vaccinations play a decisive role; together with the substances delivered up to the brain barrier via the PCR test sticks, the effects of the under-supply of the body with oxygen caused by mask wearing, the conventional vaccinations, the conventional medicines, the chemicals sprayed into the atmosphere, the genetically modified food, the administering of fluoride to drinking water, table salt, and toothpaste, the constant radio waves, and much more. Just imagine what is inflicted here on the human body from birth.

In order to open the doors to the divine light again and to let in higher frequency energies into this plane of existence, the star children have now incarnated in this final time period, with whose help all these devolutionary processes which lasted for eons can be neutralized and healed again.

Gnosticism and astrology

At this point, I would like to come back to the topic of Gnosis and the respective book about it by John Lamb Lash, which I mentioned in the first part of this book.

According to this author, the Gnostic teachings are considered to be the original Christian teachings, *i.e.*, the teachings on which Jesus Christ based His works. Meanwhile, the current interpretation of the Christian teachings is based on the canonical writings of the Bible which, according to the chronology presented by Raik Garve, were created from the 16th century onwards to serve the then forming institutionalized church and the papacy. These writings serve to keep people controlled and imprisoned in a certain spiritual worldview that they cannot escape. Man's access to God and the divine is thus only possible through the official church and its representatives. There is only one life on earth for everyone, and after that the wait for Judgment Day begins. Hope for salvation is promised by every religion for those only who join the respective group (Catholicism, Jehovah's Witnesses, Free Christian Churches, *etc.*). In this thought model, people who do not belong to these groups are unfortunately lost and will not be able to find salvation.

It is assumed that a human being is created for this one life only, that he had no prior form of existence or being and therefore no experiences before, and that after this one life, the waiting time for the Last Judgment begins for the soul of the deceased.

Thus, the human being will of course not look for any previous experiences and existences and would neither recognize nor appreciate them or the corresponding memories of it. He thus remains completely isolated from the reality of his own being outside of the current life experiences.

This is another fundamental element for remote-controlling the human creator force. The connection to one's own soul and being can thus only be attained in a dogmatic way via outside institutions (the official religions and their authorized representatives). Such religion is then almost devoid of any authenticity.

What has astrology to do with Gnosticism?

In the Gnostic writings, it is described that on the way into an incarnation, the soul must pass the archons which are represented, among other things, by the planets. Each archon/planet provides the soul with a stamp for this life, which finally becomes life-dominating at birth.

According to the Gnostics, the way of liberation lies in giving back these stamps.

All this makes a lot of sense to me, considering that we as beings have existed for a long time and that our origin lies outside of the earth sphere. Insofar, our timeless being is completely uninfluenced by the respective constellations of the planets which can be perceived from earth. Only during the time of incarnation do these planets (stamps) have an influence.

The influence of the planets at birth and through life is, according to my understanding, a prison for the soul. Certain character traits and abilities are granted as they correspond to the constellations of the planets and houses at birth, and most other talents and potentials are excluded or at least strongly diminished. In addition, there is a predictable cyclic influence on the human being throughout his entire life. Again and again, there are times and constellations that are favorable, but the "bad" times inevitably return when the planetary constellations are unfavorable again.

From this cyclicity, of course, recurring worldly cycles can be derived, even the rising and passing of cultures and communities of peoples. And the cyclicity ensures exactly this rising and waning eternally, with no escape available. On a large scale, a cyclic migration takes place over 26,100 years through the ages of the 12 signs of the zodiac, which returns earthly creation to the same places time and again, like in a merry-go-round. From the wisdom of the gnostic teachings, it can therefore be derived in my opinion that we must step out of the "soul stamps" received through the astrological influences at the time of our birth, and enter a holistic state of being. The planetary energies thus lose their influence on our consciousness and our room for manoeuvre, and we regain access to our full potential. Likewise, after ascension into the 5th dimension, there will be no return to an age of Kali Yuga.

In some writings it is noted that Jesus freed Himself from this astrological programming and exemplified what abilities, potentials, and possibilities come with returning back the "planetary stamps."

In a way, I can understand that there had to be a system that made it possible for a soul to have an individual experience. The planets with their forces ensure that there are hardly any entirely identical astrological constellations among people. If we were not subjected to theses planetary stamps, we might not be able to have the experience of complete separation from the divine wholeness. In this respect, this is maybe an aspect that has made possible the individualization of the soul and the sensation of separateness from the All-Oneness.

It seems to me that in these times, however, we are in a situation in which the return of the souls to their origin is pending, and the experiences made here are to be integrated into the wealth of experience of the whole universe. The star children have incarnated in this time on earth among the people to help, so that earthbound humanity can find its way back to its original source. This has become necessary, because there are powers here, as already described earlier, which would lose their energy source and their own framework of existence with a return of the souls to their primal ground.

Computer idealization and parallel worlds

Generally, there is a consensus in spiritual and esoteric circles that we as mankind, the earth, and the universe are moving into a higher level of vibration.

There is much talk about an ascension of earth and mankind into the 5th dimension.

How can we imagine living in the 5th dimension? I imagine it in such a way that capabilities are then available like telepathy, teleportation, nourishment by Prana energy, access to the

Akasha chronicle, levitation, manifestation by spirit power, and so on.

Also, according to my understanding, it will no longer be possible to tell lies or to deceive one another because we will be able to perceive the energy underlying a statement (as it has always been possible at least for small children). In my opinion, it will also no longer be possible to use any being against its own will for selfish purposes. We will be conscious about our connectedness to everything at any time, and thus we would partake in any suffering which we have caused others. This connectedness also exists nowadays and we also feel the consequences of our actions, but we cannot connect these consequences to their cause. For example, if we buy products that have been produced under inhumane and undignified circumstances and for which suffering and hardship have been inflicted on other beings, then this also affects us, for instance through illnesses, accidents, unpleasant circumstances at our work, or unpleasant life situations of any kind.

Nevertheless, many who are concerned with the ascent of mankind imagine that we will use the tools of our 3D plane also in higher dimensions, but in a more developed form, *e.g.*, that we will use computers and nano-technologies and the like. This idea causes a feeling of great disturbance in me. I feel that the technologies we have come to know in our present level of being serve to a large extent the purpose of our subjugation. We are controlled by them, made dependent, degenerated, and thereby are ultimately prepared for the (attempted) separation of our divine light spark from our being. Circumstances have been established in our plane of existence that have made us absolute dependent on technical resources; resources which are externally operated and controlled and which can also be switched off at will; resources that can break, that wear out and need to be replaced. I am sure that it is possible in higher dimensions to access any knowledge, any information which is available in the universe, purely by means of our mental power. As we will freely dispose of such abilities in the 5th dimension, our preparation for this leap in consciousness should also include a letting go of the concepts that were forced upon us in this 3rd dimension and in these times.

So, if the above-described higher vibrating energies dominate in the 5th dimension and our consciousness has expanded accordingly, what need would we have for computers, for instance? Would we still need such technical devices to store knowledge or to find solutions? That seems very unlikely to me. For example, crystals or quite simply the ether can be a storage medium. All experiences which were ever made are energetically permanently present. It is possible for beings in higher dimensions to tune into these "memories" if they wish, no computer is necessary for this. In my opinion the pyramids in Egypt were built without the use of computers. I think that such ideas arise from the limited understanding of the 3D world. We project our world of experience into higher vibrating worlds of experience, and we simply cannot imagine that the primitive tools of our level of existence are no longer needed there.

In the same way, it irritates me when time and again there are reports about "higher developed" extraterrestrial civilizations which are waging wars against each other and for dominion over the earth. In my opinion, an earthly state of consciousness is used here as a template for the imagination of a higher vibrating level of being, and this does not fit at all into my idea of the 5th dimension. At the most, something like this may be valid for the 4th dimension, but not for the 5th and higher dimensional levels.

Also, I wonder whether it is actually required in the 5th dimension to fly constantly through the universe with spaceships. According to my conception, higher dimensional beings are able to teleport. The physicality in higher dimensions is subjected to other laws than we can imagine in our presently 3-dimensional existence.

Prison Earth

When we begin to wish for or imagine a better world, our starting point is usually the level of experience we are familiar with.

A world with a health care system, a financial system, an energy system, an educational system, a political system, a governmental system, an administrative system, a traffic system, religions, and so on.

PART 2

Again and again, I see efforts to imagine a better world in which the social structures known to us are just further developed for the best of all.

I do not regard this as promising. Because in my opinion, all these structures were developed in the first place as instruments of domination over mankind. I do not think that a higher vibrating civilization will need these structures, because every being can take care of itself in every form. It is no longer necessary to give your "voice" or "vote" to others, who then make decisions on behalf of the people, taking away part of your own life energy in order to have it at their disposal. For example, there is no need to organize a health care system because there will no longer be such a thing as illness. There is also no need for an educational system because any knowledge can be retrieved from the Akasha Chronicle. In this respect, this new world view can only be imagined in a meaningful way if we have access to all these abilities ourselves. Otherwise, we will succumb to the erroneous belief that institutions and experts are needed for certain areas, as seems to be the case in our present society.

From an energetic point of view, our learned helplessness has led us to accept a model that keeps us completely unfree and determined by others (see my comments in the chapter "The fallacy of democracy" below).

Most of the structures that make up our society are therefore tools to keep us controllable. They have been developed for this purpose and therefore should have no place in the visualization of a higher vibrating world. That would be like changing the prison administration but not leaving the prison.

In esoteric circles, I often encounter a thought concept which says that our world will split up into parallel worlds of different vibrational levels, or has already done so.

Practically, this would mean that our common level of experience divides into many simultaneously existing levels of experience, of which then the present level continues to exist for all those whose consciousness cannot or does not want to develop further. If we call the present level of experience Earth A, then there would be, for example, an Earth B for people whose consciousness has developed a little further. Earth B would then be vibrating a little higher and thus be an improvement of Earth A. And Earth C would then exist in the 5th dimension, and all those would be allowed in there whose consciousness has developed far enough so that they can adapt to this high level of vibration.

My impression, however, is that it will not happen in this manner. And I think that this model also serves to dissuade the star children/voluntary souls from fulfilling their task.

The entire frequencies of humanity, the earth, and the universe are increasing. My understanding is that there will no longer be a frequency level that allows for the continued existence of an "Earth A" because that is no longer vibrationally provided for. That there could be an Earth A at all, has been made possible by the corresponding waves of creation. These could arise and develop in the time before the beginning of the 8th and 9th creation wave. The 9th creation wave transcends these previous creation waves, however, and does not allow such unconscious and separated states of existence any longer.

It seems that earthbound humanity cannot get out of the surrounding frequency and consciousness prison on its own, and the energy necessary for this is still controlled by the extraterrestrial powers dominating the earth sphere. Humans and their light energies are also used by these forces to build a protective shield between themselves and the higher vibrating light, because these powers would not be able to exist in those higher frequencies.

An enlightenment and liberation from this can only happen from within the earth sphere, through the awakening of mankind. And for this reason, the voluntarily incarnated souls and star children are currently among us. They can establish the connection from this plane of being into the quantum field and open the door through which the light can flow in. In this way, the divine light can finally come to the people and reconnect them with their origin. Thus, the vibrational level of the earth sphere is raised, and it is up to each individual human being to decide at this moment to let go of the old narrative. Where this willingness is not present, a leaving of the physical body will likely occur. Only this time, the soul does not go into the familiar fourth dimension but into a community with well-meaning light beings, who assist these souls on their way to their true origin. Therefore, the model of a multiplicity of versions of the earth vibrating at different consciousness levels can be excluded in my opinion.

Actual state of our life / free will

It is of tremendous importance to understand how our world and life is formed and maintained by the foreign use of our very own creative powers, and how we get entangled in "karma" without even being aware of it.

First, it is necessary to understand that in the present social system on this earth there is no real freedom of choice — no real free will.

Why?

Free will can only exist in the face and full availability of the truth. This is not possible under the present circumstances, because mankind has been maneuvered by a comprehensive external manipulation into a state in which truth can no longer be recognized as such. The resets described above, the imposed belief systems, and the various manipulations of mankind carried out over a long period of time do not allow to freely encounter the truth at present. People have been imprisoned in a system that drains them of almost all their life energy without them being aware of it. Only with the greatest possible subordination to the system is it possible to provide for essential needs such as food, shelter, and clothing. This contradicts the cosmic laws of creation, because every being in the universe is provided with more than enough creative power and connection to the infinite energies of quantum space to have a secure basis of existence in every way. The restoration of this foundation is the first prerequisite for being able to use one's own free will.

The second prerequisite is to heal all individual and collective traumatization with the power of love and light.

Only then, a circumstance occurs that allows people to make a free decision and to exercise their free will.

Since this is prevented to this day, it is necessary to energetically create as fast as possible the circumstances which make the exercising of free will possible.

Also, prior to incarnation, no free will was available because the souls of earthbound mankind are not free in the intermediate space between the incarnations, as already described above. Only the illusion of free will is maintained which, unfortunately, is not recognized correctly by many spiritually and/or esoterically thinking people.

Now, the powers which have brought the earth sphere under their control have meanwhile managed to manipulate the people in such a way that these have placed themselves as unconscious shields between the dark forces and the light. Any well-meaning intervention from the outside, wanting to end the rule of the earth-controlling forces, would also destroy mankind together with their foundations of life, since humans were programmed in such a way that they cannot distinguish the light from the darkness any longer.

This fact was made painfully clear to all of us in the past 3½ years.

People follow the given narrative in blind obedience and complete passiveness, no matter how obviously the rulers here commit offenses against them. Parents are forcing face masks onto their children and have themselves and their families injected with untested and questionable substances, "attentive" citizens denounce their fellow human beings, and the deliberate destruction of a world worth living in is being sanctioned by their behavior. It is hard to describe in words.

Hardly anyone questions whether the radiation from WLAN, 3G, 4G, and 5G networks and the use of cell phones could be harmful to the body. Hardly anyone is surprised by the strange "clouds" in the sky, although there are already public sources that admit that chemicals are sprayed into the atmosphere for the purpose of climate control. Also, hardly anyone thinks about the consequences of switching to electric-powered individual transportation.

And now there is a war in Europe, and here, too, no one questions how it could come to this but only blindly follows the one-sided reporting of the mass media.

For many years now, I have had the impression that in conversations I am no longer talking to the authentic essence within people, but to a programmed entity. Most of the topics, opinions, and views I encounter are based on narratives propagated by the mass media, and habits that have been instilled into us. This also includes basic beliefs, e.g., what is worth striving for in life, how to deal with health problems, where those come from, and so on. People accept the invisible mental walls that are our prison in this level of being and energize them without being aware of it.

At this point, it is necessary to put the global narrative on pause and to create the space and framework so that all manipulation, traumatization, and programming can be lifted for everyone, at least for the moment of decision-making and the exercising of free will.

And after this has happened, this level of being will move in its entirety to a vibrationally higher-dimensional level. Depending on their individual decision, people will join this, or they will choose another way back into the light.

Once this is done, then also the presently lived out dark narrative will be over. And following this caesura, healing can take place on all levels and for all entities in the earth sphere.

It is exactly for this purpose that the light-workers and volunteer souls are here. And this book shall bring about that we remember this together and implement this together *now*.

Where are we : not

Now, we should deal for a moment with our present life and its energetic consequences.

The starting point for us in western society is that we believe that we live in a free, democratically organised society. We assume that we are free to choose a profession according to our preferences and inclinations, and that it is in our hands to do good in the world if we want to.

But this hardly works for anyone, even if we want to pretend that it is so with much effort. And this is because we either consciously, or rather predominantly unconsciously, ignore the interconnectedness of all of existence, we only look at the surface but not at what lies behind it, and we vehemently defend our model of life out of self-protection, because otherwise we would lose our grip on life. This is all very understandable, I do it just like everyone else. Nevertheless, we all must look behind the veil and face reality in any form, even if it hurts and scares us, even if it destroys the beautiful image that we have built up of ourselves and that others have of us. Without this step, we will not gain the understanding necessary to completely disengage from this world model, and to open ourselves joyfully, freely, and consistently to the divine light that makes our being and existence possible.

This will be a moment beyond all concepts, a moment that will carry us into another dimension.

So, what does the current situation look like?

We all go through a basic programming. First, after birth, we are shaped by our adult caregivers. However, it begins even before birth because in the womb we perceive everything our mother hears; conversations, television, cinema, music. We perceive energetically what is read and thought by our mother. And in recent times, we are also penetrated by the waves and signals that are emitted by transmission towers, cell phones, WLAN, and so on. Please visualize for a moment that in these radio waves the entire contents are included which are transmitted by them. Such waves are no directional signals which go specifically from the transmitting station to the receiving station, but they are always scattered over a wide range.

Let us imagine that the pregnant mother is sitting in a café in the city. In this environment, countless cell phones are in operation, there are WLAN networks and radio and television signals, plus the many radar transmitters in cars for the respective assistance systems and, of course, GPS and other radio signals of which we know nothing. All this transmitted content now reaches the mother and thus also the unborn baby. This content includes violence, pornographic and hateful themes, war, and other fear-producing topics.

We, the voluntary souls who incarnated in the early 60s to the early 80s of the previous century, were not exposed to this imprinting to the same extent as children are nowadays. In addition, today's food is even more degenerated than it was a few decades ago, and of course, in the meantime, evermore food has been genetically modified. Even if "only" the feed of farm animals consists of genetically modified corn or soy, this also enters the human body via meat, milk, and egg products. We eat food that has been heated in the microwave, food in which all cells have been broken and therewith all living nutritional content. This also separates us from creation and prevents our physicality from being in harmony with Mother Earth.

Later, we are subjected to up to 15 years of mind programming and brainwashing through daycare, kindergarten, and school which continues even further when we go to college or university.

Prepared in such a way, we enter professional and adult life.

If we take the trouble to look which effects our job has on the earth and the human community, then we would soon find out that we cause mostly damage in some way or other, and that we have no real influence on the behaviour and actions of our employer.

If, for example, we are employed by an automobile manufacturer and would look at where and from whom all the raw materials and components for the vehicles that we produce are coming, we would very soon conclude that many processes are not humane and environmentally sound, because parts and materials come from countries that allow for the environment and people to be exploited without restraint. We would find that even in our own plant, conditions prevail that are not acceptable. If, for example, we were to enforce that the supplier products are designed and manufactured transparently and in a completely humane and environmentally compatible manner, then our company would have to discontinue operations, simply because our vehicles would suddenly cost many times more than those of our competitors. And if all our competitors ran their businesses in the same transparent and humane way, we might not be able to afford a vehicle ourselves under the given circumstances.

The same goes for food. There, too, our employer will, for the most part, use practices that do not meet the highest standards. For example, in Germany there are limits on the concentration of pesticides in vegetables or fruit. Each of these agents has its own limits, and we may even comply with each single limit. But instead of one pesticide on the lettuce there might be nine different pesticides, all of which comply with their individual upper limit. But nobody has investigated what it means to eat vegetables that have been treated with nine different poisons.

I mention this only as an example. If we are mercilessly honest with ourselves, then almost all of us will find that in our field of activity, there is a similar situation.

Let us now look at "nobler" professions, such as yoga teacher, homeopath, spiritual advisor, energy healer, astrologer, mental coach, or similar. Perhaps we can confirm for ourselves that we are working according to the highest idealistic standards. But can we also offer our services to all the people who work for our own well-being, *e.g.*, on construction sites to build our houses, and at the checkout in the supermarket where we buy daily necessities? People whose income is barely enough to cover their basic needs and to whom we would have to provide our services almost for free? Do we ignore this? Or do we justify this by saying that it is these people's own fault that they earn so little, just so that we can have exclusively wealthy customers?

But what do our wealthy clients do in order to be able to afford our services, how do they earn their money, and who generates their income? Perhaps those very people who cannot afford our services themselves? And what impact do our clients' activities have on other people in the world? Are people in Asia, Africa, or South America perhaps working under inhumane conditions so that our client can earn a good income? And by accepting this money, are we not also involved in this process?

I would like to cite an example from our time in Canada. At the country's largest drugstore chain, a software program had been developed that determined exactly how many employees were needed at any given moment for each store based on the daily and weekly sales distribution. This data was made available to all franchisees with the proviso that the individual weekly hours of the employees had to be adjusted in each case to the presently determined conditions. In other words, the employees were now given completely arbitrary and irregular weekly working hours, which led to a noticeable reduction in salary. The store manager's comment on this situation: "No one here can rely on fixed working hours anymore, and whoever wants to have that should please look for another job."

What if a programmer, who has developed such a software and received a lot of money for it, takes a luxurious yoga class with us? And what if we know that his work has just worsened the lives of 20,000 employees of the drugstore chain so that they can no longer even think about a yoga class, because they now must see how to maintain their essential income via a second job? We are all in some way entangled in such an externally controlled and resources-abusing network.

Again, this is not at all about badmouthing your life and your world view. But if we do not face the truth and the reality now, then this dark world system advances further with our direct or indirect approval. Our world is built the way it has been built precisely for the reasons described above, so that there is no real escape for anyone. At best, there can be a mental escape by suggesting to oneself that one's own behavior does not contribute to the suffering of others.

In addition to our own work and professional environment, our own consumer behavior is particularly important.

With the financial means made available to us and their use, we set in motion unimaginable processes worldwide every day, or we sanction and support existing processes. We usually have no influence on these processes and on what we use our money for, because we also make our decisions to a great extent based on the way we were being programmed.

This form of mind control begins at home, continues throughout our school years, and is supported by television series, movies, computer games, news broadcasts, billboards, and so on. The so-called "advertising" is in principle a highly psychological manipulation and deception. Thereby, by means of psychological methods, customer needs are specifically generated for things that no one really needs. Since our world and society are built in such a way that we are cut off from our essence, our meaning of life, our origin, and our life energy, we permanently live in a deliberately induced deficiency.

The paths we would have to take to compensate for this deficiency and fill the deficits have been systematically closed to us. Thus, we are an easy victim for advertising campaigns, because these connect those attributes which we desire and need so urgently, with absolute senseless and useless products. In this way we burn through clothes, computers, televisions, cars, furniture, technical devices, cell phones, electrical bicycles, and cosmetics; we buy and buy and never come to rest, never arrive anywhere. In addition, we constantly feel the pressure that our purchasing power, even the ability to cover our essential needs, is latently endangered at any time. If we do not play our part in the big game the way we are expected to, we quickly slip into circumstances that can threaten our very existence.

And here again as a reminder

Upon our birth, we bring with us any resources, any ability, and any capacity that we need for our life and our physical existence, each one of us.

And we all make the experience that these assets have already disappeared shortly after our birth and have been transferred to other entities (see also my remarks in the chapter "The concept of tomorrow"). According to the rules which the masters of this world have set up or had set up by their henchmen (heads of government, parliaments, public administration), we are given back only a small fragment of this energy for our services, and we are then allowed to spend this small fragment to try to fill our original deficit in a mentally manipulated way.

If we would like to create a larger free space for ourselves, then this can only be achieved (directly and indirectly) by taking away some part of other people's life energy. How else can it be that a programmer is royally rewarded for his working time, but a person who works just as much time or even more in food retailing, receives only a fraction of this amount? How is it possible that a person who teaches yoga, or the like, earns more income than someone who must work in road construction every day, exposed to the weather, noise and dirt, and in a toxic environment?

This is not about further endless discussions or the question whether I am right with my thoughts just a little bit, for the most part, or not at all. It is about feeling from the heart's point of view whether there is something wrong in this world. And indeed, there is. We have now come together here through this book in order to put this entire worldly structure into the light, in such a way that the truth comes to the surface and the universal forces and laws can apply here again.

The use and application of our financial means

Each expenditure of money sanctions unimaginably complex processes. For example, if we buy a car, this car has come into being from a very large number of individual processes, starting with the extraction and manufacture of the basic raw materials such as steel, plastic, wires, textiles, *etc*. We have no way of knowing whether the steel, for example, was produced in areas of South America where secondary forests were cut down to fuel the blast furnaces for smelting, and how the people used for this were treated. The same applies to all other components of the car. Nevertheless, by buying and using this vehicle, we are inevitably drawn into a partial responsibility for all the production steps involved. This is an energetic fact. We now have the option of renouncing everything we cannot follow up from A to Z, or to awaken. Awakening seems to me to be the better solution here.

What we must stop doing is to whitewash our actual influence on world events. By doing so, we only build up an artificial defense that allows us to regain our supposed peace of mind. The volunteer souls and light-workers are not here to judge humanity. They are here out of connectedness and gratitude for the task that earthbound humanity has taken on through many incarnations. They are here with their whole being to express the gratitude of the entire universe to humanity, for what humanity has taken upon itself and achieved here. If we allow this thought, then we can forgive ourselves first and then forgive others, and immediately thereafter turn our focus to the light and our return to the light, freely and joyfully.

The fallacy of democracy

We have all been led to believe that we need institutions that make decisions for us, in our name and with our authorization. However, from the very beginning we have only very limited parts of our inherent wealth at our disposal. And even from this limited and always endangered portion, a significant part is taken away from us by these institutions. If you look at the qualifications of those who make decisions on our behalf as representatives of these institutions, it can turn your stomach. The culmination of this can currently be observed in Germany, but this also finally makes the whole system visible in all its tragedy. Decisions are made that cause catastrophic circumstances and conditions. In addition to the resulting damage, the money (= life energy) stolen from the population is subsequently transferred to other states and wealthy businessmen. We as electorate are helplessly at the mercy of this. No matter where we make our cross on the ballot papers, we can be sure that by the party structures exactly those are made electable, and are elected, who obediently maintain the global narrative and who have already given their consent to decisions which were made way in advance from a much higher level.

Democracy is just as much an instrument of domination as are monarchy, communism, and similar structures. People who will never be accountable to us personally decide on almost every aspect of our lives, and are supported in their external representation by the centrally controlled media. As long as these supposed decision-makers obediently do their job, they are under the global protection of the powers that control them. If they give rise to the assumption that they no longer want to remain unconditionally obedient, then there are many ways to stop them.

According to my understanding, after our awakening and the energetic ascent into the 5th dimension that goes along with it has happened, there will be no more structures that control and command other beings by using their life energy. Therefore, none of the usual institutions and structures of our world's society can exist anymore, simply because the truth can no longer be hidden in the 5th dimension, and our world can currently only function by hiding the truth.

"Healthcare"

What we understand under the term "health care system" is basically an industry which can be called a disease system. The very foundations of knowledge on which this industry is based only allow those involved to nurture and create disease.

First, it would have to be recognized that illness is generated by deliberately creating circumstances that deprive people of access to their true being; circumstances that mentally cause people to have dysfunctional thoughts and emotions, to continually damage their physicality through the kind of food they ingest, and to surrender their sovereignty over their own well-being to artificial authorities. Dysfunctional thoughts also include information about illness and health that we absorb from the media, then internalize, and then share with others; and likewise, the thoughts which are introduced to our mind by the participation in preventive medical examinations. These "screening programs" are nothing more than business creation models of the "disease system," whose operators are aware that our own mindset and mental attitude to our health have supremacy over our physical condition. When our belief in our health is strong, then we are healthy. If our belief is characterized by doubts, fears, anxieties, and is dependent on the judgment of external authorities, then our state of health follows suit. And the disease system makes use of exactly this circumstance. It cleverly plants thoughts and convictions in the human mind which reinforce each other, and thus create illness.

If we stay conscious of these circumstances, then the disease system will collapse very quickly. There is no more place for it, neither in the 3rd nor in the 5th dimension.

What we know as medicine (except homeopathic remedies as well as purely herbal preparations without harmful additives), contains chemical substances and additives that do not belong in the body. These substances are harmful poisons which burden the body and purposefully cause more disorders, which are then treated with further pharmaceuticals. Although here, too, the faith of a human being is capable to neutralize almost all the harmfulness. So, if we unwaveringly believe that a doctor and pharmaceuticals are the solution to our health problem, then this will probably be so. It is only our belief that causes this. But would it not be better to believe in the first place in ourselves and in our divine creator energies, and with these creator energies immediately visualize and bring about an awakening for all of us? To come right to the point: Exactly this is what I want to do together with you, and for that I am writing this book and visualize that you read it for that!

Industrial branch "disease management"

All participants in this branch — doctors, hospitals, pharmacies, pharmaceutical companies, health insurances, and screening laboratories — make their living from the fact that the number of "sick" people remains at least on the existing level, or better, that it increases because then there is more turnover. Almost no one in the disease management system can seriously wish that their "services" are no longer needed by people, because then they would become redundant in their current function. Therefore, for their own survival and for the continuance of their own activities, they need the sick ones. The powers dominating the earth sphere can therefore rely on the fact that a mindset is being imposed on the populace which ensures that they create within themselves through their belief sickness that the disease system then may cash in on. Disease is one example of how well mind control has been implemented for ages that effects all of humanity. Basically, the potentials of the 6th and 7th have been used to ingrain a collective mindset in all of humanity that now controls the bodily functions in a predetermined and degenerative design. One could say that the genetic modifications of the human body by alien interference have been given permanency through the mental manipulation of humanity, as described above. Through the process of awakening, we can immediately reverse this programming and bring our bodies back into perfect harmony. Especially the energies represented by the 9th wave of creation can be used to counteract all forms of genetic manipulation.

By lobbying, it is achieved that mainly treatment methods are chosen which are profitable for the disease management system, and it is ensured that health insurances pay for extensive screening programs which generate new patients with their outcomes. The "screened" people then share their experiences with their environment and thus set in motion mental symptom manifestation processes in a correspondingly sensitive part of their fellow human beings.

And of course, the entire disease management system is based on medical training. This is designed in such a way that the business model of illness always works well. Thus, suffering is generated, maintained, and nurtured. An artificially fragmented and manipulated view of the human being is conveyed, and only when this has been adequately internalized does a graduate receive the authorization to work in the system as a doctor, pharmacist, or the like.

What is completely ignored are the subtle bodies and levels that make up our earthly existence, besides the visible physical body. It is ignored that our food must nourish not only our physical but also our subtle bodies. Due to industrialized agriculture and processed food, the human being is no longer provided with a nourishment that serves all physical levels. The resulting deficiency expresses itself as "disease" — as disorder — which of course cannot be treated by a system that completely ignores the causes. It should be obvious that under these circumstances no conventional treatment method can bring healing.

Example Vitamin D

We are advised by the disease system to stay out of the sun during noontime (from 11 a.m. to 3 p.m.), and ideally to use a sunscreen the rest of the time. If we consider that the body can only produce enough vitamin D at midday, with larger areas of the skin exposed to the sun, then the above advice makes little sense. If we also consider that the eyes of our body are a gauge for the intensity of UV radiation and that this is how our body activates its protective mechanisms, then it becomes clear what influence the wearing of sunglasses with UV protection has on the natural reaction of our skin to solar radiation. With sunglasses, the risk of getting a sunburn is therefore much higher than without wearing sunglasses.

Without our body's own vitamin D production, which in our northern latitudes can only take place in summer and with the corresponding exposure of our skin to the sun, our susceptibility to infections is always high. If vitamin D were supplemented to a sufficient extent, our susceptibility to respiratory diseases, for example, would be significantly lower. If we stay out of the sun in summer, this almost inevitably leads to a permanent vitamin D deficiency[‡].

[‡] See the research work of Prof. Dr. med. Jörg Spitz.

AWAKENING

In this "healthcare system," some essential components of our 3D existence exist on the side lines, such as emergency care, treatment after accidents, holistic dental care, or personal assistance for psychological problems without the use of medication. Such segments still would remain in a first step of streamlining this branch, and of course all those who carry out their work with idealism and love for people. But this is about our ascent into the 5th dimension. In order to get there, it requires the willingness to be open for the truth. And it also requires the willingness to leave the systems of the 3D world behind.

I myself have worked in a pharmaceutical company, in a government agency, and in a company that sold souvenir items, many of which were produced in sweatshops and third world countries under degrading conditions. The point of my comments above is not to criticize the people who do their work in this system with heart, soul, and the best of intentions, nor to get them to justify themselves and their field of work. We do not know the entities and beings that have created this overall system in which we live, nor have their intentions and goals been clearly communicated to us. However, if we want to complete the path into our awakening and the light, it is necessary to face reality and to draw consequences from it. This is what it is all about now, and I would like to offer some assistance with this book.

Through our "education," we have already received a completely distorted understanding of our being and have thus internalized belief models that are directed against our own body system, since we ignore countless aspects of our being and are in disharmony with our own existence. This is also a driving force into illness. Our body communicates with us trying to wake us up, which then leads us to entrust ourselves even more to the disease system, which only makes everything worse.

And on top of it all, there is the greatest manipulation of all, the supposed aging. As if it were a god given consequence of life that body and mind deteriorate and lead to a loss of vitality and life force. This is not so.

Even in the case of regressions to former existences outside the earth sphere, the clients, when asked about their age in the respective life form, often give values that are based on current life expectations on earth. In my opinion, this is a sign how deeply the traumatization from the different global resets has been burned into the collective human existence, since even here on earth, lifetimes of several hundred years were common in earlier advanced civilizations.

The causes for our aging are our social programming as well as a downright warfare of this manipulated world construct against the integrity of our being. This warfare also includes our working world; more about this in the next chapter. We are being "burned out" throughout our professional life, only to be transferred subsequently from home care to institutional care as "care cases" with gradually increasing necessities. This is also a booming industry. The operators of care services and care facilities are concerned with generating as much income as they can, and with generating the highest possible profits with underpaid, performance-optimized personnel. Those who lose the most in the process are the care patients and, of course, the nursing staff.

How much suffering, despair, pointlessness, and hopelessness is generated here? What kind of image of man and what kind of image of God do we have that we believe in such a narrative and consider it to be true?

We are all star children, and this kind of life is not only not worthy of us, but we are committing an offence against each other if we continue to believe this false story to be true. And we will not solve this problem by trying to improve our way of life with expensive alternative cures or medicinal preparations for the wealthy. We need to wake up from this dark dream.

The world of work

We live in a world in which our needs are mostly met by corporate entities and by processes that have been broken down into many separate parts.

As employees, we have almost no influence on the way our company conducts its business, and our employer, due to the existence of competitors, is always forced to keep up with price competition.

In order to increase profits, globalization has been driven forward. Companies that used to manufacture in the US and Canada until the 1970s, were able to realize enormous cost savings by relocating working steps to Asia. This initially brought them high margins, until this business conduction became suddenly necessary for the companies' survival because a downward price war ensued. Thus, one industry after another disappeared from North America, and only the brand or trademark remained. The production itself though was subcontracted to manufacturers abroad.

In addition, there was the "discounterization" of the retail trade, especially in Germany. The Aldi company and subsequent discounters transformed grocery stores into sober warehouses, placed goods on shelves in shipping boxes, reduced the product range considerably, ensured that only disposable packaging was used, even for beverages, and were thus able to massively reduce the need for staff. This model then also allowed the discounters to deal with suppliers in a completely new way. The latter either had to comply with the price and quality specifications dictated by the discounter in question, or risk economic ruin by losing the business relationship with this client. In addition to food, the discounters began to expand their product range into the non-food sector, and there too the prices of specialist retailers were aggressively undercut.

In North America, a similar effect took place through the widespread expansion of Wal-Mart, only they would focus in the beginning on non-food items of all kinds and would only later expand into the grocery store segment. To understand how radical the discounters in Germany operate, one must recall that Wal-Mart failed to get a foothold in the German market, as they were simply not able to compete with discounters like Aldi.

For us as customers, this was simply wonderful at the beginning. We saved ourselves money while shopping and were able to consume much more overall. Of course, we did not save on our car as we now had even more money left over for that.

What we did not realize was that the people in our neighborhood and community who worked for Aldi's or Wal-Mart's supplier companies and in the industrial sectors, whose production was relocated to Asia, suffered a severe loss of income or were being laid off. As a result, our own employers also had to struggle with a drop in sales and a loss of business, since income that could have been spent again was destroyed. And in this way, we pulled each other into a downward spiral which finally went so far that nowadays temporary employment agencies are becoming more and more dominant as our employers. People are treated only as a thing that is used and needed sometimes here, sometimes there, and sometimes not at all. From the money which is paid for the deployment of the temporary employee, first the time-work agency helps itself before the actual employee service is honored. This is also a model that does not promote the self-esteem of the employees and their mental and physical health.

For me, however, there are some even more important questions.

How can it be that work is always scarce, that as a worker you always must fear for your job, even if it is not fulfilling? That if you lose your job, you must chum up in a humiliating way to get a new one? That employers are almost always in the driver's seat?

What if…

- we manufacture every product with maximum durability? So that, for example, household equipment can last for 25 years without having to be replaced?
- we do without any form of advertising and psychological manipulation, and on the contrary, would strengthen people psychologically so that they find their meaning in life beyond possessions and products?
- we localize the world instead of globalizing it, and greatly slim down the large administrations of governments on all levels and even abolish them for the most part?
- we completely renounce the production of cheap disposable goods?
- we only use free energy sources (no more wind and solar power, too)?

In this way, a large part of the current "work" — one can also call it forced employment — would no longer be necessary, and we could approach life much more relaxed and harmoniously.

It would certainly be possible to add many more examples and topics to the ones given above.

Summary and continuation

At this point, I would like to suggest that we together build a connection between the different thoughts and ideas that have been considered so far, in order to successfully walk and celebrate the path of awakening together.

It has been established that the soul beings that make up humanity have embarked on a journey into a lower vibrational and more solid existence. At the beginning of this journey, it was naturally possible for the souls to change from an earthly form of existence back to a higher vibrational level of being. At first, these incarnations in the earthly plane of being happened in such a finely vibrating manner that there was no leaving behind of the remains of the physical body. The human body which gradually became denser with time could be dissolved and left at the self-chosen and self-decided end of an incarnation. Thus, one will not find any human physical remains from these times, they simply do not exist. A new re-incarnation was possible at any time, however always voluntarily.

Analogous to the already discussed changes of the creative vibrational levels (according to Carl Calleman/Mayan calendar) and the accompanying changes focusing the light energies of creation on the whole existence (male/female both in the light and no separating duality present, male in the light and female in the dark, and vice versa), always new forms of existence have developed. From the 5th wave of creation on, the human souls began to incarnate into an ever more materialistic and dense physicality. Up to approx. 12,000 years ago, a holistic consciousness still dominated because the 5th creation wave shone its light equally on both sides of existence. With the approach of the 6th creation wave and the darkness coming with it to those aspects by which the female side in the universe is characterized, however, a new main emphasis in the earthly human existence began to emerge.

"Advanced civilizations" arose which carry, *e.g.*, the names "Atlantis" and "Lemuria" in our memory. It is difficult to make reliable statements about the exact periods. I would assume that the Lemurian "advanced civilization" could have taken place between 20,000 B.C. and 15,000 B.C., the Atlantean one afterwards until about 12,000 B.C.

Why do I put "advanced civilization" in quotation marks?

From our today's point of view, we would regard these cultures as advanced civilizations, since these still had a very close connection to their mental forces and the use thereof, and with these they could create completely different physical creations than we can today. No effort comparable to today's strenuous creative processes was necessary. Everyone could provide themselves effortless with their existential needs, and the intake of physical food was at that time certainly not compellingly necessary. It can be assumed that balanced climatic conditions prevailed on earth, and that generally a constant spiritual contact into higher dimensional levels and to the respective spiritual families existed. There were no "diseases" and no "aging."

Nevertheless, these cultures were already the expression of an evolutionary process into an ever lower vibrating form of existence, into an ever-denser physicality. In this respect, these cultures were a transitional stage from a purely spiritual form of existence into our present dense and unconscious form of embodiment. Lemuria was still in the consciousness of wholeness, and Atlantis then developed into the preliminaries of the 6th wave of creation.

I assume that in this state of more and more condensed physical existence and our increasing difficulties to remain conscious about the aspects of our own origin, those dark powers and forces have entered our plane of existence to begin with the implementation of their plan which is today in its final moments. We are presently experiencing a decay of values and a destruction of everything that constitutes humanity, divinity, love, and respect for life, that would have been unimaginable to me in this form 3 years ago, although in fact we have been in a war against humanity for centuries, if not millennia. Nevertheless, the result of the manipulation and influence of the foreign powers now becomes apparent in a way which was probably not perceptible before. However, the "Spanish flu" directly following the First World War certainly has many parallels to the present time, and the former great "resets" also had catastrophic effects on human existence. Regarding the "Spanish flu," remember that the first worldwide "vaccination campaign" preceded this event.

When I first read Dolores Cannon's book about the three waves of volunteers, the content already made great sense to me. I have already spoken about the role of these souls incarnated from all levels of the universe. Nevertheless, it was only in the past 2½ years that it became clear in every form why this action was absolute necessary. Until then, it was more of a mental concept for me that earthbound humanity would indeed not be able to find the way into the light in time and on its own. Also, until the year 2019, I myself felt in many aspects as belonging and being part of this earthbound humanity. I always found enough overlapping areas of interest and could maintain a free and enriching exchange with many people.

Since the beginning of 2020, however, a caesura began in which the vast majority of earthbound humanity has succumbed to the dark spell that has been woven around it for thousands of years in such an all-encompassing way that I can hardly grasp it.

I am writing these lines at the beginning of July 2022. In these days, the topics of genderization, the handling of the Ukraine war and its consequences, but also the still dominating Corona narrative are being pushed in such a shocking and sick way, politically and in the media, that it becomes obvious that most people have now been brought to the point that they go along with any agenda, however malicious and dark it may be.

And it is this very circumstance that is now forcing the star children and voluntary souls to awaken. Now the essence from Dolores' book about the waves of voluntary souls suddenly makes sense to me in any way. Without these voluntarily incarnated souls, earthbound humanity cannot be awakened.

So, we experience today how comprehensively and proactively these times have been prepared by the earth-dominating powers over eons. And I cannot imagine that these powers would make such a gigantic effort in order to be stopped shortly before reaching their goal. They surely provided against all eventualities which could threaten their plan.

This precaution becomes apparent also in the fact that

innumerable variants were placed among the futuristic conceptions of esoteric-spiritually inclined people and their interpretations of the current times. There is a frequent agreement with the idea that redemption, liberation, transcendence will take place sometime in the future. There are mental models according to which humans still have a longer learning time ahead of them, and there is even the idea that it still requires a whole series of further incarnations in order to become ready for the light. These ideas assume a viable further existence of the earth and biosphere. This includes of course the vehicle "human body" as well as its nutritious requirements. And these presuppositions are just being eliminated in an alarming way, because the earth-dominating powers do not need a functional earth sphere any more and act accordingly.

We have already spoken a few times about people's manifestation powers. Spiritually inclined people also know about this and guide us in being aware of the effects of our thoughts and words, and our emotions and feelings. Exactly in the same way, however, it is also true that most people who follow today's artificial narratives are using the same creative powers with their thoughts. If we look at the state of the world today, we can see what comes out of this. It is frightening that most people do not draw any of their own conclusions and knowledge from it, but interpret world events by what the mass media feeds them. The resulting programming is shared in conversations between people as if it were their own wisdom. Thus, it is understandable that the esoterically inclined humans see parallel worlds as the only way out at the end, based on the concept that many humans still have a long path of development ahead of them and that they have decided "freely" to continue remaining in this dystopic world. This thought model then also contains so many other esoteric branches with often contradictory conclusions that it seems to me like a perfect model of mutual obstruction. Unfortunately, most of these ideas and insights are very much influenced by the present level of experience which is the result of the preceding cataclysms. It is necessary for the voluntary souls and star children to remember their true being, and to release themselves from the collective traumatization stored in the human body.

AWAKENING

To prevent the disastrous development described above, it requires the awareness and awakening of the light workers. In the presence and light of a higher vibrational level, neither the current global agenda nor the beings perpetuating it can continue to exist in the present way. To what extent these beings and powers can in some way also follow the path into the light is still unclear to me. This may be possible, but it would require a great change from the beings concerned.

We can therefore state that we are all solidly bound together in an artificially created reality of life, which has succeeded in separating the whole of mankind completely from its connection to its own origin and level of being. Instead, an artificial reality was created and energized which locks us into a very limited framework of life. This artificial frame was brought into being by the abuse of the creative power already stolen from humans at birth. It is maintained and further developed by constantly drawing off the bits of life force still remaining in people's lives or given back to them in exchange for work.

During different resets and the catastrophes resulting from them, the frame of consciousness available to the people was constantly limited further. It is noticeable how certain aspects of development of the two highest vibrating waves of creation, the 8th, and the 9th wave, were taken up by the earth-dominating powers and were directed into specific channels. We already talked about our telepathic abilities which were shifted to the use of smartphones. In such a way, it happens presently with the necessary coming together of the opposites in people and the inner integration of the masculine and feminine aspects of being. This issue is a prerequisite to establish the connection to higher vibrational levels and to channel energies and realities from these levels into the earthly realm. Thus, it becomes apparent why the topic of "genderization" suddenly takes such a central place, despite so many crises threatening our existence at the same time. Precisely because a transcendental opening into the light will emerge from the inner union of the male and female aspects in us, this significant topic has fallen prey to utter alienation and manipulation.

Parallel to this, especially in Germany, the mass media are providing new thoughts to the population to be energized. And thereby existential fears move more and more to the center of attention.

Will I still be able to heat my home in winter?
Will there be enough to eat?
Will there be enough electricity?
Will I still have enough financial means to cover my basic needs?
Will my house have a forced mortgage?

And many more. In addition, of course, the next freedom-robbing measures are imminent by supposed further waves of virus variants, and then somewhere there are monkey pox, and a latent fear of an escalating war is also lurking in the background.

With these fears, enormous mental forces are released in the collective which in my opinion are meant to override any finer vibrating energies and concepts. These fears are another key element in the portfolio of the powers ruling over us, who want to prevent our awakening. If at the same time many spiritual models assume that we still have enough time for many more incarnations to perfect our being here, or that, if necessary, we will depart from unconscious humanity into other vibrational levels when things turn bad, then this all plays to the plan of the rulers of the earth. It seems to me that such spiritual concepts may even be launched intentionally, to be used as a controlled meeting place for the star children in which their potential is then neutralized.

Flat Earth?

Ever since I have moved to Paraguay, the topic of a "flat earth" comes up more and more often. Until then, I assumed without any question that the earth is certainly round, as this can be seen on numerous photographs taken from space. Satellites are launched into orbit, there is a space station, probes have been sent to other planets, we orbit the sun, and the moon orbits the earth. That still makes sense to me today.

However, I personally cannot invalidate some of the arguments of the proponents of the "flat earth" theory. Especially, that over certain distances on the earth's surface one can see objects which, from the point of view of the observer, should have already disappeared behind the curvature of the earth, or that even from an airplane one cannot perceive a curvature of the earth, and that the horizon of view is always in the center of the field of vision and does not disappear downwards. However, this is also not a topic which we should discuss further here in technical detail.

But suppose we were told that an ignorant and spiritually not very advanced mankind had in ancient times succumbed to the naive belief that the earth represents the center of creation and that the heavenly bodies circle around the earth.

Then, someday, a notion comes from the Freemasonry that this is a wrong assumption. The earth is a round celestial body which has ended up by chance in a very favorable orbit around the sun, which offers by chance very favorable conditions for the development of life. A little closer to the sun and it would be too hot, a little further from the sun and it would be too cold for that. And on top of this, the earth is now to be perceived as smaller than a dust grain within the space of an infinitely larger universe with innumerable galaxies.

Of course, this has changed mankind's self-image of their existence and the significance of the earth's sphere dramatically.

As long as the earth was the center of the universe, its importance was great; everything turned around the earth, not only physically, but also from a creative point of view. When the earth suddenly became a speck of dust in an endless wide space, man lost his footing and the reference to his own significance.

Today, people discuss again whether the earth is perhaps flat, and they bring forward arguments which cannot be invalidated so simply and easily.

So, let us only once assume that the earth was flat. What is the case then regarding the planets and other celestial bodies? Where exactly would they be? Maybe much closer to the earth than assumed? And would these planets possibly have been placed at the firmament to exercise the archontic powers for controlling the people? Exactly those archons who put stamps on us on the way into incarnation, which we must give back according to the Gnostics if we want to become free and whole?

Many concepts and worldviews would collapse, even in the spiritual community, if the earth were flat.

One more thought on this: What kind of coincidence is required that a small celestial body close to the earth, *i.e.*, the moon, has almost the same size in the visually perceptible firmament as a celestial body that is vastly more distant in comparison, but many times larger, i.e., the sun? And that the two precisely cover each other time and again in the form of eclipses in the sky? That is truly a gigantic coincidence.

Food for thought.

I would say at least that the topic "flat earth" needs another debate, because there are too many inconsistencies with the globe model which would have to be clarified.

The mission

Just how much sophisticated misinformation has been taught to us is no longer relevant. It is important to understand that the world we perceive around us has been artificially created to function as a prison for the human spirit and the human being. And unfortunately, besides the institutionalized religions, there are also many branches of the esoteric-spiritual community among the originators of such misinformation. Many hypnoses regressions, spirit journeys, and psychic messages are distorted and changed by the artificial frequency frame of this level of existence. Sometimes they are only baseless fantasies, and sometimes they are robbed of their essence, just as it is the case with the general existence of earthbound humanity because they also have no access to their essence anymore.

And at this point, I turn to the voluntarily incarnated souls and star children. You have entered the earthly world of experience in order to create the energetic framework that allows earthbound humanity to regain access to its essence, to its true being. For you were aware that people cannot find their way back on their own, and that they did not know at the beginning of their entry into this experiential earth space ages ago how the circumstances would unfold here. If it would have been clear to them, and if they would have been able to foresee this current kind of existence on earth which we all experience together now, then they would not have had to make these experiences and they would have known how to get out of this situation.

AWAKENING

My thoughts, then, can again be viewed and discussed from many angles, different models can be discussed, and so on. And afterwards, they can be put aside in order to focus once again on a never occurring future.

Earthbound humanity is now relying on the voluntarily incarnated souls and star children to make the way home accessible to them again. We do not achieve this by focusing on well-off clientele and by offering workshops, treatments, and spiritual retreats to them on a small scale. Such clients are often engaged in furthering the agenda of the earth-controlling powers and receive remuneration for this very activity, which allows them the luxury of an esoteric-spiritual treatment or coaching. By catering to such clientele, we will not be able to fulfill our task.

It is the humans living meanwhile in ever greater unconsciousness, and who mostly find no access at all to esoteric and spiritual topics, for whom we are here in the first place. And these people, across all age groups, are now given a compulsory therapy (mRNA treatment) which leads to ever more serious changes in the biology of their body and which blocks their soul's connection to the universal light currents even further. Incredibly strong negative energy fields are being created through these large masses of people and the steering of their mental focus, which condense around the earth (be it flat or round) like an armour. Because of this armour, no more star children will be able to come to earth, and if the three waves of voluntary souls and star children who are currently incarnated do not fulfill their mission, then further incarnations of light beings do not make sense anymore. The precautions taken by the rulers of the earth ensure that there will no longer be a framework for the incarnation of light beings who are yet foreign to the earth (and who have had no prior incarnations). Mankind, which is already now hardly conscious anymore, is then no longer reachable due to all the measures of the past centuries - and particularly those just being carried out.

And thus, I consider a thought model to be very questionable which concludes that there are people who are more qualified to ascend into higher dimensions due to their consciousness level than the majority of mankind, which still has to do many laps of honor in low-vibrating levels of experience. Apparently, it has been possible to convince many light workers that they are "better" than the masses of people, due to their prior soul work, and therefore are allowed to "ascend."

The light-workers have entered this level of experience especially for earthbound humanity in order to keep their part of the agreement with the earthbound people. These people have entered a realm of experience which did not necessarily require that they would one day find the way back out of this frame of experience on their own. The light workers differ from the earthbound humans in that they came here voluntarily and well prepared in an express process without karmic entanglements. But they did not come in order to go right back to where they came from. If that had been the goal, they would not have had to come in the first place.

This situation looks to me like a deliberate steering away of the voluntarily incarnated souls from their mission and therewith from what is happening on this earth plane. From the work of Senya Kandoussi, which is based on the QHHT regression and hypnosis techniques developed by Dolores Cannon, I gather that apparently numerous of the voluntary souls have incarnated here as avatars. This would mean that their own body, which they inhabited in other dimensions before the beginning of their time on earth, continues to exist there in a sleeping and preserved state. Only a part of the consciousness of these beings is currently incarnated in a human body. After the earthly death, the animated spirit immediately returns to the other dimensions and to its original physicality. What a realization it would be when this soul, on its return, would find that it has lost itself in the mental games of the earthly plane of experience in such a way that it has returned to the starting point with unfinished business.

Hence my urgent feeling that we now need a complete and unrestricted awakening of the voluntarily incarnated star children.

What we should become aware of is that there are hardly any concepts in the spiritual framework that foresee an ascension of the earth and the entire ensouled humanity. There are many different models, but time and again they contain the element of leaving behind a large part of the earth's population in various low vibrational versions of our present sphere of experience. Often an ever more developed computer technology is supposed to make life better then.

In my opinion, these scenarios serve the purpose to propagate an island of gloom which can only be left by a minor part of mankind. And an inner feeling tells me that such an outcome would have repercussions on all dimensional levels of the universe.

My impression is that nowadays many of the voluntarily incarnated star children are worn out by the experiences in this dysfunctional 3-dimensional world. And only those still appear empowered who have succeeded best in coping with the structures of this level of being, often by earning their living by offering spiritual services of various kinds. Certainly, this is a relief and support for a certain number of clients, but it could not prevent the present worldwide development and its effects on mankind. Only in very rare cases, people can be assisted in such a way that they can free themselves from the clutches of the world agenda. And that is because all of us remain largely contained in the frame network which the rulers of this level of existence have defined for us.

This frame network is characterized first by the fact that we have to make use of the limited resources of this plane of existence. In this framework, we define our goals and pursue them according to the predetermined rules.

Occasionally, somebody succeeds in using the creation framework of the quantum field, but primarily in order to realize their own earthly goals more easily.

Basically, the frame network can be described as follows:
- We are limited and defined by our physicality. This physicality is highly vulnerable, which means that it must be protected from weather, needs constant nourishment, and is susceptible to disturbances (diseases, injuries, old age).
- We need to play a role in the social/economical system that allows us to acquire sufficient financial resources to meet the needs of our physicality.
- Our food and goods production are predominantly manual. It is done by institutions that siphon off large amounts of money in the process; through large scale agricultural

food production (from conventional agriculture to artificially produced food in factories) or through construction companies (a 3D printer, *e.g.*, is also a manual production process, only here more technology and fewer people are deployed), garment factories, automobile factories, power plants, construction and maintenance of wind turbines, road construction, sewer construction, waste disposal, huge trade structures, transportation companies, *etc.*. These are all manual processes in which humans must involve themselves compulsorily, in order to be able to cover only their own basic needs.

- In this model, the best paid are those who create and maintain the framework for the management of humanity through this system. First, these would be all those who command these processes such as the owners of the largest companies (*e.g.*, Amazon, Wal-Mart, Apple, Volkswagen, Bayer), those who manage and control the life energy (flow of money) of mankind (*i.e.*, private banks, politicians, WEF, Bilderbergers, central banks, *etc.*), and those who are responsible for the opinion-making (the entire media sector including communication media, such as social media). Right at the forefront is also the IT sector. Due to the rationalization of work processes, people are laid off and are often forced to look for lower-paid and simpler jobs. This maintains the artificial scarcity of work, driving people into mutual competition for jobs and forcing them to twist their own personalities. Rationalization through IT processes does not lead to a more pleasant life for the same number of employees, but rather to the opposite.
- Nearly everyone must use the artificial system described above to a certain degree in order to make a living.
- In such a system, it is possible, desired, and respectable to use other people for the attainment of one's own prosperity and, on top of that, to reproach these people for being responsible for the fact that they did not generate better living conditions for themselves. This concept has also been taken up in the book *The Secret*. Whoever does not make the cut, that is their own fault.

- And here I remind you again of the already discussed topics. We all act in this manner, each in their own way. Even if we do not directly employ people who make our own prosperity possible through their work, every single item we buy has been created from this system. People are exploited in one way or another to make this product for us. And our own clients and customers, in turn, are involved in processes that provide them with an income, a portion of which they give to us in return for our services.
- We are not able to provide for ourselves on our own and independently. A self-sufficient way of life is not possible for us, and if attempts are made in this regard, projects come out of it which burden the participants with many restrictions and efforts, *i.e.*, they become so difficult to realize that this is not an option for most people. We can see this in all the countries of the world, also in developing countries, that people are not at all or only with great difficulty able to live satisfactorily and to provide for themselves.
- In this system, it is indispensable for people to return time and again to the "disease system," because their denatured mental and physical way of life regularly leads to physical and mental disturbances. This "sickness system" can only be used with correspondingly available financial means, so people need at least a job in order to have insurance in the system. The disease system is promoted by propagating and providing denatured food, radio waves, pollutants in any materials, unhealthy work rhythms, noise, stress, *etc*. This also includes advice that is detrimental to health, as discussed earlier in this book in relation to the vitamin D production in the body.
- The entire construct of the supposed history of our planet and of humanity which is presented to us is one of the foundations of the frame network, especially in relation to our origin, potential, and possibilities. While there are countless spiritual directions that contain all kinds of beautiful thought models about our being, the fact always remains that we cannot access our true potential and that we cannot detach ourselves from the frame network.

This list is certainly incomplete, but I think it can give you a basic idea of the frame network in which we are caught.

As long as nobody leaves this frame network, everything is "allowed." Therefore, there are no perpetually stable products, no free energy, no type of education that enables humans to develop their full potential, and no generally accessible and above all generally affordable energetic healing methods (we would need these only transitionally because used correctly, they would enable the clients to connect with their own inner healing forces, so that in the future, they would not need any external assistance regarding their health issues).

Here again a circle closes, because our "awakening" includes stepping out of the constraints and limitations of the frame network. And as soon as we do this, we are in direct and unfiltered touch with our soul families and higher parts of consciousness which are waiting, so to speak, at the gate between the worlds for us to open the door from the inside. Because only then can they enter our earthly plane of being and become effective. That is why there are the voluntary incarnations, because these souls represent the whole of humanity, and in their embodiment, they can re-establish the connection to the source for all of us. As soon as this happens, the karmic concept is dissolved and our consciousness will no longer be in such a limited frame as nowadays on earth.

PART 3

OUR AWAKENING

Transformation

In the first part of this book, I have mainly dedicated myself to the narration of my life path so far. Perhaps to remind myself, perhaps because it can show you parallels to your own life, perhaps also so that it becomes clear which influences I was exposed to before writing this book.

What I experienced on my path often evoked resonances in me, activated my own thought processes, and led to spontaneous insights. Time and again, I took up a topic and reported my thoughts on it to my wife. And while I was doing this, the topic was unfolding in me in ever new and more complex facets. I just went on and on, and my insights emerged as I spoke. Where these insights came from, I cannot say. It is not so that there is a being contacting me, or that I go into a meditative state that enables some kind of transmission. While I speak, the contents simply arise. And in doing so, they further develop my previous insights and build on the existing ones. We even got the idea that, when I began to talk in this way, we should turn on a recording device to be able to later write down my thoughts in a collected form, maybe in the form of a book.

This did not happen, and only in the past two years, when our world began to go off the rails, the feeling came up in me that it might be helpful to write down my thoughts. And that is what I have done in the second part of the book.

This book was certainly not written in a way that is common for other authors. I just sat down and started writing, without a concept, without a structure. I trust that there is more than just the superficial content woven into the written words, that there is an energy that reaches out to you on a deeper level and connects you with it.

Thus, the second part of the book contains many insights that came to me spontaneously while writing and which combine all the information I encountered with intuitive insights of my own.

I am aware that in a rational discussion of the contents I have shared so far, there is much that can be controversial, and some of my views might be outright rejected.

However, it is not my intention that in the end every single topic is discussed as a fragment, but I would like to draw an overall picture which offers enough comprehensible clues to sensitize you as a reader for the conditions and developments on our earth in such a way that you can get out of the present world narrative with your entire being, and it is my intention that we do this together and thereby connect our creative forces back to our origin and bundle them together.

This morning, I came across a comment on the Internet which referred to an article about the emergence of our modern "disease system." The article talked about how the modern "disease system" was created in the USA by the Rockefeller family after the end of World War II. The aim of this system was to replace all natural healing methods that had been used until then with synthetic medicines from the petroleum industry (chemical industry). In order to be able to implement and realize this as quickly as possible, the Rockefellers began to finance the institutions that trained physicians. In return, these institutions had to turn unconditionally to chemical medicine and remove all alternative healing methods from their curricula.

As a result of these new forms of treatment and chemical preparations, cancer incidence began to rise significantly. In order to prevent any unpleasant conclusions in this regard, the Rockefellers founded the Cancer Society. And with that, the business field was expanded because under the guise of searching for a cure for this disease, only the handling of this disease was institutionalized. A gigantic new branch of business was created. The causes were concealed, and early detection programs were set up to attract patients. This is also the origin of all private or state programs under the guise of the "fight" against cancer. Immense amounts of money are collected, which in turn benefit only those who make money from the expensive treatments and preliminary examinations.

In a similar way, the entire "disease system" was also used for today's Corona narrative. The comment I mentioned above concludes with the following words: "*I have faith in Team Humanity 1.0. The 99.9999999%* are depending on you to wake up from your sleep quickly and get into action.*"

* "of the people who follow the narrative" (my annotation).

I myself hope that Team Humanity 1.0 is larger than the author of the commentary assumes; however, very large it is not, and you are reading this book because you belong to that group of people on whom the big remainder of humanity now depends. We have talked about this subject in detail in previous chapters.

This third part of the book is a call to recognize and connect ourselves on the soul level beyond our earthly personas and characters. It is important that we find ways to do this without ego collisions which can arise very easily, especially among the star children of the 3 voluntary incarnation waves. We are all currently at home in a world that not only does not correspond to us in terms of vibration and experience, but which is highly overburdening us in many aspects. It is difficult for us to find our own role in the community with which we can take care of ourselves. Some of us have succeeded only to a limited extent, and we are involved with employers and in work processes that run counter to our inner being. We sometimes must pretend in order to be able to integrate ourselves into society. In doing so, we have often built a mental framework all by ourselves that allows us to survive in the greatest possible mental and spiritual health in this unfamiliar and hostile environment.

Some of us have managed to find their livelihood and centering in the spiritual field, and in this way, they can earn a living as counselors, teachers, or by sharing their knowledge through social media and the like.

And this is where things start to get tricky.

On the one hand, a steadily growing part of humanity has been provided with mRNA preparations, in addition to the physical and mental consequences of social distancing and wearing masks. On the other hand, it is also foreseeable that very soon there will be no more freely available financial means for people. These will at least be allocated by the controllers in such a way that they can only be used for certain permitted purposes.

Thus, our income would soon be generated either with clients who support and have submitted to the manipulated narrative or, if we remain true to our heart and soul mission, then it may no longer be possible for our clients to pay us, since they might no longer be able use their then only digital funds for our services. At least, if we remain true to ourselves, there is a high risk that we would have to look for another vocational activity.

It is also time to question whether our activities and what we offer our clients are only intended to make the current situation more bearable for them, and whether we are ultimately unable to offer people a perspective for a life beyond the constraints of the narrative. For example, if our clients can only generate their income by wearing a mask all day and having test sticks shoved up their noses on a regular basis, or if they are possibly even losing their job because they do not want to be treated with mRNA preparations, what can we offer these people that will free them from this situation? Can it be enough to just give them a little comfort in exchange for payment?

Is it not rather probable that in such a way we are forced all together on the way which the earth-dominating powers have planned for us? And is it enough if we withdraw into thought constructs aiming at a wonderful redemption in the future, at a new Golden Age that is constantly postponed to new starting dates?

Have we not hoped and waited long enough for moments in the future? I think so. It is now necessary for us to find, open, and pave ways for the light of truth, love, and awakening to reach us. It is necessary to open doors through which our light families can enter this level of being. It is now time for us to awaken.

The field

Earlier in the book, I mentioned that at the end of our time in Mexico and immediately after our return to Paraguay, I encountered the work of Dr. Joe Dispenza. In the meantime, I had the opportunity to investigate his work a little further.

Dr. Joe had a very serious accident as a young man during a bicycle race. His spine was so badly injured that, according to all the experts he consulted afterwards, the only treatments available to him were those that would have left him permanently disabled. No one could offer him an alternative form of therapy. Dr. Joe decided not to undergo any conventional treatment. He had to lie on his stomach most of the time and began to imagine what it would be like to be able to resume his previous life. Because of his medical training, he had a very good idea of the anatomy of the spine and what his injured vertebrae would look like in a healthy state. So, after a few weeks he began a mental routine of working his way forward vertebra by vertebra, visualizing them in detail in a healed and intact state. He then developed this visualization over time to the point where in his mind and imagination all the vertebrae were healed and he would be able to resume his normal life. And after a few months, he had indeed managed to heal his injuries to the point where he could stand up and walk again. He also was determined not to wear a brace, although his doctors thought that that was absolute necessary.

After six months, Dr. Joe resumed his usual life. He had managed to heal himself with the help of his mental power and his connection to the quantum field of unlimited possibilities.

Building on this and incorporating the classical sciences, Dr. Joe has made this method public in books, lectures, and seminars over the past decades, and the participants of these events achieve similarly overwhelming results.

Dr. Joe Dispenza points out that the longer we live, the more we live in a physically internalized past. Over time, our body becomes dependent on the chemicals that are produced by it as a result of certain emotions from the past. For example, by remembering unpleasant moments from our lives, the hormones associated with the original event are released in the body just as they were at the time of the incident.

This refers, for example, to all situations in which we have been treated unfairly or maliciously, such as a breakup with a partner after many stressful situations, bad treatment by our parents, an unpleasant dismissal by our employer, cheating by friends or a spouse, or the like. On all such occasions, our body has released stress hormones. According to Dr. Joe's research, it makes no difference to the body if an event is actually happening or if it is just remembered. It reacts chemically-biologically in the same way in both cases. And our memories of such events increase more and more, and with them the opportunity to relive them again and again, along with the corresponding hormonal reactions of our body. Over time, we become addicted to these hormones and the sensations they cause, and our bodies keep transporting us back to those long-ago moments of stress through memories of the respective events. At the age of 35, according to Dr. Joe, our thinking is 95% dominated by the events of our past, and we can face new situations and problems with only 5% uninfluenced free brain capacity. It is easy to understand that in the end we have locked ourselves up mentally.

In other words, we live with our body in a constant stress-filled state of emergency, which it cannot cope with. Normally, our physical reactions to stress serve to provide a particularly high physical responsiveness to the corresponding circumstances in life-threatening situations. However, this must later return to a normal state so that the body does not suffer any damage. Unfortunately, with increasing age we live more and more constantly in such exceptional states, and the corresponding disease syndromes are derived from this which in turn are treated with chemical drugs that put even more strain on the body.

In the way described above, we checkmate each other with the life circumstances sanctioned by us and passed on to new generations. We lock our entire being into an emotional cage that encloses ever larger aspects of our lives as we age. Social media and digital communication tools play an important role in this. They bind our attention to an ever-increasing extent in our increasingly sparse "free time." Thereby we learn and deepen the consensus reality imposed on humanity more and more. This consensus reality shapes our thinking, and the life circumstances that derive from it determine our emotions, our well-being, and our health.

Dr. Joe cites several studies that show that the very focus on which we direct the power of our mind causes physical effects. An example: For one study, two control groups were formed. All study participants had their wrists put in plaster for four weeks so that they could not move them. The first group did strengthening exercises with their wrists for 11 minutes on 5 days a week, but only mentally and not physically, because the wrists could not be moved. The second group did nothing of the sort. After the casts were removed, the muscles in the wrists

AWAKENING

of the first group were twice as strong as those in the second group[†].

Such examples could be easily continued.

It is this power of our mind that shapes our external and internal reality. So, let us once again keep in mind how our world level is controlled. The key factors are the thought models that dominate us and determine our understanding of our being and the supposed laws of the universe. The realities of life that result from these thought models prepare the ground for our confinement from birth into limiting and repetitive thought models that keep us trapped in our past, and cause us to create our future based on our past experiences. We function more and more on autopilot, so to speak, each additional year of our life. The bad thing about this is that at some point in our lives, we all have traumatic experiences in some area, which from that moment on are repeatedly energized by the memory of these experiences and thus have damaging effects on our physical health, on our way of interacting with other people, and on the quality of new experiences. According to Dr. Joe's research, we project our past experiences into a foreseeable future. Personally, as well as collectively, we thereby energize the world in which we live every single day.

We have seen many examples of this in the second part of the book.

Studying the work of Dr. Joe Dispenza has once again confirmed to me that we can create or change just about anything we want by means of our mental power. First and foremost, we can transform our physical existence on all levels into an ideal state characterized by perfect harmony and health. In principle, we do not need any external help for this, although in the beginning certain techniques, such as reiki, can help us to reach this state of complete inner harmony. I am convinced that this also includes the topic of aging. For me, "aging" is an expression of being broken by life. Our life experiences put more and more strain on our physicality, and the accumulating negative memories have a correspondingly severe effect on the health of our physical organism.

---

† See page 38 in the book *Becoming Supernatural* by Dr. Joe Dispenza, published by Hay House.

PART 3

In the insights of Dr. Joe, I see a key for our awakening together.

Awakening : now

Hopefully, we can understand quite well by now why an awakening of earthbound mankind is not possible without the help of the voluntarily incarnated star children. We can also understand why up to now, even these voluntarily incarnated beings have lost themselves in the mental prison of this earthly realm in one way or another. Precisely these beings are often more affected by the psychological pain on their path through life than earthbound mankind which is energetically better attuned.

Nevertheless, the star children bring along a decisive advantage. As soon as they meditatively go into the quantum field, they can gain access to the memory of their life's mission and to their higher self. Also waiting there to get in touch with them are their spiritual families and their spiritual companions through this life.

I would like to invite all readers of this book to do so. We now have the opportunity to connect with each other on the soul level and to bring the frequency increase for the ascent into the 5th dimension from the quantum field into our present level of experience. Thereby, frequencies enter our earthly world in which the artificially created and low vibrating world models of the earth-dominating powers can no longer exist. The transhumanist goals can no longer be pursued and our entire plane of being can be healed. The special thing about it is that this will happen during embodiment, in fact, for all beings that currently exist on earth in physical form. And in this way, all experiences ever gained on earth can benefit the All-Oneness of the whole universe.

What happens in the end and how it happens when we ascend together, I can only speculate about here. What is important is that an "ascension in the body" occurs, which has been foreseen by many of the indigenous peoples of the Americas for these times. And this process is unique in the history of the universe.

My intention in writing these lines is that they are not only directed to your earthly consciousness, but also to your Higher Self. Thus, it is also my wish and hope that not only my earthly limited self is writing these lines, but my Higher Self gets involved.

What can we do together to let the change into the light take place on our level of being out of the quantum field as fast as possible?

I think that in the first place, we should increasingly and as far as possible withdraw from the conventional mass media. Then, and this is already more difficult, we should also consider well which alternative media we still want to follow. We should particularly avoid those that repeat the contents of the mainstream media in order to criticize, expose, or discuss them. Because with this we remain, whether we like it or not, integrated into the current world narrative. In this way, the information reaches our consciousness after all, and thus we cannot avoid energizing this narrative because it is hardly possible to withdraw from these contents, since we know about the specifics of the collective thought world of the manipulated people. It seems important to me that we energize and create together our own new parallel reality with our whole being, and for this purpose I would like us to form a group of like-minded people who will come together and bring about a resonance field that reconnects this realm with our joint source field, and by that reverse all manipulation that has happened to this realm of being and to earthbound humanity throughout the past thousands of years. More on that later in the book.

At the heart of our work together should be our connection with each other and with the quantum field. I would like to recommend the book *Becoming Supernatural* by Dr. Joe Dispenza, which provides the technique and a deep understanding of how we can detach ourselves from our pre-programmed way of life and together build a connection into the quantum field. Through this connection, we should together, whenever possible coordinated at the same time, direct the higher vibrational energies for our awakening into this level of being. I imagine that we connect ourselves in meditations with the quantum field and from there initiate our awakening and the corresponding vibrational changes on earth. For that, at the

PART 3

end of this book I will provide a vision of the changes which we effect thereby.

To those of you who are reiki givers, or who know reiki givers who are open-minded towards our shared project: you should give yourselves reiki as regularly as possible, or have it given to you, and thus dissolve the blockages that have so far prevented us from our awakening. Reiki is, in my opinion, a form of quantum healing.

We should start to regularly communicate to higher spheres our intention and readiness to awaken, be it in the form of prayers or by directly addressing our Higher Self.

There is another important aspect that has recently become clear to me, and that is the issue of cyclicality. This cyclicality is in my understanding both a general rule and an instrument which was used during the past 5,000 years (6th creation wave), in order to capture mankind in cycles which always have golden times and light, followed by dark, metallic times and shadows. This is true for the Vedas as well as for Chinese and Western astrology.

We should keep in mind that the 6th wave of creation already began to make itself felt more than 10,000 years ago. Carl Calleman refers to this as the "pre-wave." Then, 5,000 years ago, this wave began to have its effect in all its power, and the main characteristic of this wave is duality, expressed by the preference of the male side and the neglect and later conscious suppression of the female side. The Vedas and similar teachings also correctly reflect this condition and draw valid conclusions from it for the time of the dominance of the 6th wave of creation. This means that duality was given a central role in the models of wisdom and creation that emerged during the 6th wave. Good and evil, light and dark, poor and rich, warm and cold, winter and summer, yin and yang, all aspects of duality or polarity formed the dominant world of experience during the 6th wave. And from this, the wisdom laid down and experienced during these times was derived. Because this wave of creation, with its energy and power, dominated not only the earthly realm of existence, but the entire universe. And thus, the concept of cyclicality and duality is also contained in the wisdom teachings that came into being during the 6th wave of creation.

Since 2011 however, with the 9th, universal wave of creation, a new force transcending the previous waves has become dominant. For the first time since the beginning of the pre-wave of the 6th creation wave, the 9th wave casts again the divine universal light equally on both sides of the brain, equally on the male and female aspects.

The ever more increasing dysfunctionality in the world is an expression of being out of sync with creation, which we are currently experiencing here on earth. With almost all areas of life experiences, we continue to be rooted in the 6th and 7th wave of creation and bypass or distort the 8th wave of creation (light on the female side and darkness on the male side), *e.g.*, expressed by smartphones and IT technology instead of telepathy and teleportation, by masculinized women in leadership positions, such as former German chancellor Mrs. Merkel, as well as by a complete exclusion of the 9th wave of creation.

In the whole classical wisdom and religious teachings, especially the 9th wave of creation is not considered at all. As well-intentioned as any attempt is to explain the present catastrophic development of the earthly society and biosphere and to point out solutions for this situation from this level of experience, based on the teachings developed during the 6th wave, so fatal in its effects is this attempt. Thereby we serve the powers still controlling the earth by maintaining the duality and the karma principle, even if we do so with loving intention.

To be clear once again: In this way we mutually block the way out of the present situation for each other, because we do not take the decisive step. We hold on to imposed "traditional laws" and are far away from any synchronicity and harmony with the universal energies.

It may become apparent from this that this state can only exist for a limited time, that at some point the dam will break and holistic light and high vibration will flood our earthly sphere in such a way that this will dissolve our plane of existence. However, this dissolution from the outside is not supposed to be the way to achieve the ascent of earth and mankind into the light, but instead out of the existing incarnation.

This fact is not known to the wisdom teachers from the classical religious faiths and to people in general, but the powers dominating the earth plane are very aware of it. They act in a way that clearly shows that in their models and considerations, a further existence and above all survivability of the 3-dimensional earth and the biological kingdoms and life forms existing here is no longer included. The foundation of physical life is intentionally destroyed, because their goal is the harvesting of the light sparks of the souls in the context of technological developments (*e.g.*, transhumanism). These forces are aware that the ascent into the 5th dimension is to take place from within the embodiment, and as long as they successfully prevent an awakening of the light workers, they can continue to implement their own plans uninterrupted.

Therefore, in everything we are currently experiencing, one of the main goals of these powers is always to prevent the light-workers and star-children from awakening. This includes methods of sabotage such as spreading countless misleading information, views, future projections, interpretations, and so on. A jumble that prevents the voluntarily incarnated souls from remembering their mission and their true being.

Only if we, deep in our hearts, become aware of these facts, we can understand what it means to awaken now. It means above all to become an embodiment of the universal 9th wave of creation with our entire existence.

In this respect, I would also like to suggest that we focus together in our meditations and visualizations on the activation of the 9th wave of creation in our level of experience, and turn away from the diverse thought models of cyclicality. For the birth of the light and the 5th dimension into our earthly plane of being, it is not necessary to fly into a photon field. The light of the 9th wave will connect us with the entire universal knowledge, and all speculations and assumptions regarding our origins will no longer exist because then this knowledge will be always equally available to all beings.

Jesus Christ is credited with having said: "That which I can do, and more, you can do also."

For me, this has already become a key sentence many years ago which enabled me to understand why Jesus incarnated into the earthly plane of existence at a time when His work was not yet supported by the cosmic waves of creation; on the contrary. Therefore, it was subsequently possible to manipulate

His teachings and to integrate them into the presently known forms of organized (Pauline) Christianity. My understanding is that Jesus at that time brought the spiritual seeds, which can now germinate and flourish in the light of the universal 9th wave of creation, into the experience level of earthbound humanity, and possibly especially for the voluntarily incarnated star children, so that it is easier for them to access their potentials in the sense of the above quoted statement of Jesus.

Let us imagine that all these star children awaken at the same time into such a powerful potential. Thereby, we would have found our way out of the dysfunctionality and increasing meaninglessness of daily life. It is for this that I write these lines, so that together we remember our mission and the meaning of our being here. I imagine that we come together, meditate together, energize a vision together, and thus bring it into being and in this way also awaken together. I envision that we will connect with one another and will become able to form a group that will become able to for the most part disconnect from the manipulated surface life we are leading and begin to form resonances that will enable us to change our vibration in a way that will reconnect us with the realm that has been erased from humanities perception. By doing this we will form from out of our bodies a resonance with the bodily existence of all human beings incarnated at this time. Through this resonance the spirit of humanity will reconnect to source and all deception will end at once. This may sound far fetched but this is exactly what we came here for to do. Our group will need to include not only spiritually advanced members but also those of us, that took upon them to raise substantial worldly funds, because those will be necessary to facilitate the disconnection from the cages our daily lives form. To get into touch please use the e-mail mentioned at the end of this book or go to my homepage that will provide you with my contact information. I also imagine that we involve our inner dream power and ask it for dreams that guide, strengthen, and support us as a community in our project.

In the following chapter, I describe my vision for this awakening and the experience level that arises from it. I think it is not relevant whether each of us has a slightly different focal point in this. What is important is that we support and encourage each other together on the path of awakening. Once the process of awakening begins, our level of perception and understanding will expand to such an extent that pretty much all ideas that are in harmony with the light will become reality. Therefore, I hope that in my vision I cover enough aspects so that in the end, all of us can find ourselves in it to a certain degree.

Vision of the new earth and the awakening into the 5th dimension

What can we manifest from the quantum field as our way into a higher vibrating living environment on our earth?

First, I see each of us as a gateway through which the high-vibrational 5th dimensional energies will spread circularly around us into our environment. We are like lighthouses that simultaneously radiate light-filled energies all around us in all directions. These energy fields expand and finally connect with each other. In this way, larger and larger interconnected areas of light are created. If, for example, your light field expands out from Minneapolis, MN in all directions, then it connects with other energy fields that emanate, for example, from Atlanta, GA, Phoenix, AZ, Portland, OR, and so on. I trust that in this incarnation we have been spatially placed with each other in such a way that we can form a large wide field of light.

Everywhere this energy field reaches, the energy vibration begins to increase steadily. Imagined figuratively, it is as if the whole of the country had existed for centuries under a dense blanket of clouds reaching down to the ground. One sees a world in which there is only gray, a gray sky, gray waters, gray nature, gray humans, *etc.* The rest of the earth is just as gray. And even the sages who left us their teachings found the light only beyond the reality of the physical earth experience and told us about it in their writings and traditions. Thus, our conviction has formed that we can find the light only somewhere out there in other levels of being and experience.

Wherever a star child directs high air pressure (symbolically speaking) from the quantum field into their environment, the mental cloud cover begins to dissolve steadily. At first, more light penetrates through the thinning but still closed cloud cover, but soon the first blue spots appear in the sky, until after some time the sun shines on the world around us from a brilliant blue firmament.

From the point of view of our entire environment into which our luminous energy field is spreading, something is happening here which, according to almost all traditions and wisdom teachings, can only take place through hard work, a long journey through numerous existences/incarnations, or in places far away from the earth.

For the people who dwell in our light portal, the challenge is now to be able to accept this light, and to bear to look at themselves and the truth. This is about an allowing of the light and a letting go of the previous level of experience and existence. I imagine that the light that we radiate into our environment, by letting it flow through our earthly existence, is changed vibrationally in such way that it touches people by means that allow them to survive the transition into the 5th dimensional vibrational level, first mentally and then also physically. This is one of the main reasons why the voluntarily incarnated star children have chosen such an authentic way of existence on this plane in these times.

The light-filled vibrations that we radiate into our surroundings naturally reach not only humans but also all other realms of existence, such as the plant, animal, elemental, and mineral kingdoms, and the ethereal worlds. Until now, these were dominated and deformed by the controlled collective mental energies of humanity. The high vibrational light now enters all these aspects of life and immediately begins to transform them accordingly. This also directly affects the quality of the air we breathe and the water we drink, as well as the vitality of all fruits and vegetables we ingest. Thus, a process of transformation begins for the people, working from within and from without.

The light energy emitted by the awakened star children into their environment can also neutralize all harmful technical and energetic facilities. Since the light energy penetrates all levels, it does not even stop at weapons depots, chemical storage facilities, wind turbines, radio transmission antennas, and the like, and these facilities are neutralized in such a way that no more harmful energies can emanate from them.

Bodies of water, plants, animals, whole landscapes, and the atmosphere are purified, harmonized, and healed.

A special and intense effect will be the removal of the dense veil which obstructs the truth. Awakening will always be accompanied by truth. Our present level of experience has been shaped by the obscuring of truth and the suppression of the ability to perceive truth. In the light of truth, our present dysfunctional world cannot continue to exist.

It therefore also becomes clear that the light workers who, through their very being, enable these light portals to emanate around them, do not have to convert anyone to anything or convince them of anything. In this respect, our mutual activity is rather a passive activity. We guide the light through our portal into our environment and the light does its work. In a world of darkness, suddenly the light comes on, and this must be embraced on the part of humanity.

As much as we presently have to put up with concepts and assumptions, we will not need them anymore as soon as the flow of light from the quantum field through us into this plane of existence has begun. Just by our common and simultaneous connection into the quantum field and our shared vision and common orientation, it will increasingly be revealed to us what the 5th dimensional living environment on earth will look like. It will help us if we share the gained impressions with each other and include them in our future meditations. In this way, our focus and our channel into the light will become evermore clearer.

The light spreading through us will quite soon begin to awaken people who are particularly receptive to these energies. These may be more star children, but also people who are fundamentally more open to such fine vibrational energies. These in turn can help the people in their immediate environment on their way into the light.

Our common work will therefore from within lead to quiet, peaceful, and loving changes in our level of being. Just as we have planned it for this lifetime.

Doesn't that sound as if there should be no problems or resistance?

AWAKENING

But there might be, because certain ways of life and forms of existence will no longer be supported in this higher vibrational world. Thus, after the vibrational increase, it will not be possible to use any being against their own will, neither directly nor indirectly. There is also no need for unconditional basic income or other alms to have a livelihood. One's own livelihood is always, and in every form, secured by one's own access to the quantum field, in a lightful and holistic way. No paid employment is necessary for this.

During the transition to this higher level of vibration, it will be possible for the awakened souls to have an active healing effect on all expressions of life. Here, too, the energies and frequencies used for healing will come to the earthly realm of experience in a specially dosed form, since they will be filtered through the embodied star children. The healing is energetically moderated in such a way that it leads to a gradual, life-sustaining increase in vibration, which the biological manifestations of the earth can keep up with. Thus, it becomes possible to offer to other people any form of healing by energetic means, in a way that Jesus already exemplified during His lifetime.

If this light would reach us directly and unfiltered from the outside, then the contrast would be so great that the physical life forms could not adapt to it fast enough.

What will be revealed immediately is which powers currently dominate, direct, and control this level of existence. And this is exactly the reason why there is such an extensive control of the human experience and mental world, and why it is so extremely difficult to find each other in these times and together connect with the creative light forces in the quantum field. It is ultimately the main goal of the earth-dominating forces to prevent this from happening, and for this purpose, they use all opportunities to direct and manipulate the collective creative forces of humanity.

It is important that we focus. Right now, I experience the world as restless and chaotic. An orchestra of dysfunctionality plays its symphony incessantly and prevents us from focusing and coming to rest. This challenge must be mastered, and the technique of meditation which Dr. Joe Dispenza offers us, seems to be an ideal tool for this.

In all our actions, we must be conscious that we are acting in love and communion with all of existence. What happens through our actions lies in the loving hands of our divine origin, and the energies that we bring and direct into this world will resonate with all forms of existence and life in an ideal way.

What else needs to be considered?

The previous chapter ("Vision of the new earth") represents the essence of the message for which I have written this book. In that chapter, I reveal my innermost being and longing and share it with you.

Until today, I have tried through many encounters to share my thoughts in conversations with people. From time to time, I notice that I touch people and make them reflect a little more. Something in them resonates with what I say and reacts positively to it.

Nevertheless, it is almost always only a small moment in which a window opens towards the light, but closes again shortly afterwards.

It is painful to watch how thoroughly the earth-dominating powers have prepared themselves for these times, and with how much intelligence and foresight they have readied themselves for all eventualities endangering their plan. One could say that they are always a few steps ahead of the respective situation. This is also the reason for the almost unmanageable variety of channels on YouTube, Telegram, Twitter, and other social media that supposedly accompany us through these times in an alternative and spiritual way. That also includes supposed hopefuls like Q, Donald Trump, or Vladimir Putin, as well as special planetary constellations, the photon belt, a resurrected German Empire with an emperor, and much more. We do not need all this any more. These are all aspects of the prison world that has been built around us by the powers that are currently ruling the earth.

A major component of this prison world is that humanity has accepted the belief that external institutions such as governments, the military, the medical system, the financial system, IT technology, *etc.* are needed to organize, run, and provide for society. On top of that, we are supposedly dependent on cosmic or planetary conditions that always limit our opportunities in certain places and in certain areas.

Because of this, almost all people imagine models of the future only based on their previous life experiences, and these are, as already discussed before, dominated by the 6th creation wave with aspects of the 7th creation wave. In all imaginable models of the future, certain aspects are excluded, particularly those of the 9th creation wave. Thus, people listen to me attentively and are obviously touched by my words and ideas, but then they fall back again into the mental structures of the existing world and see no possibility of a true way out of the present misery into an enlightened way of being. And this is true, too, from the point of view of the earth-bound people. With the tools and options of the existing world, a way into the light is not possible. That is precisely why the world has been built and created in this way. It even goes so far that there are time and again various reports, channelings, transmissions, and the like which extrapolate the prison construct of our present earthly existence into the conceptions of higher dimensional levels of experience. "Up there," there are still fights and wars, military commanders, warships, rulers, councils and governments, which carry out the conflicts of the earthly experience level with much more developed methods and advanced technology.

These thought models represent, according to my understanding, no correct reflection of the realities in the higher dimensional vibrational levels. Such thought models prevent us from stepping into resonance with the vibrational qualities of the 5th dimension and from enabling the transition of our level of experience to this dimension.

Therefore, I would like to ask you to read the previous chapter ("Vision of the new earth and the awakening into the 5th dimension") again and again and to remember that our vision cannot be achieved by using the usual earthly societal structures. We must leave these behind us. People who define their entire being within these structures, must also let go of them in the incoming light from the quantum field. In this process of letting go, we light-workers can ultimately also be of help, but for this the higher vibrational dimensional energy must first flow freely into our level of being.

Unfortunately, a strong deification of the digital world has prevailed among the younger ones among us, and for them it is unimaginable to ever be able to do without it again. Intuitively, however, I reached the conclusion that these technologies have already led to a very significant diversion of our inherent mental capabilities onto digital devices, and that these devices are only the prelude to connecting our brains and entire bodies to digital networks (transhumanism). Digital networks of any kind will always remain vulnerable, but most importantly, they allow for an ever-increasing monitoring and control of the users, up to the point where remotely controlled implants can be used to end a person's life at will.

Already the repeated mass administration of graphene oxide and nanoparticles by means of the mRNA treatments, and the capability of these materials to resonate especially with 5G signals, leads to the realization that most people in the western world can significantly be manipulated, directed, and influenced by this from the outside. The founder of the WEF, Klaus Schwab, recently announced in a frightening manner that the Covid crisis would only be over when all people had received a "vaccination." Then, there would be no more resistance to the global agenda.

In my opinion, one of our goals should be to reduce our dependency on digital infrastructure. This will no longer be needed after our awakening; on the contrary, the negative effects on humanity caused by these technologies will then require healing. After the awakening into the 5th dimensional energies, it will become obvious which technologies, if any, are still needed. It will also be apparent to everyone for what purpose the technologies introduced into our 3D world are actually intended.

Closing words

I am aware that with this book, with my statements and views, I may be going out on a limb in many respects. I do not float through the astral worlds or refer to masters who have initiated me. And probably, I step on the toes of some readers with my opinions.

Even if I cannot present any "proof" for my findings, I can

nevertheless make clear how unwaveringly the world-dominating powers continue with their plans and how little can be done using conventional means to stop them.

On the one hand, the transition from 3D to 5D is quite easy. And on the other hand, it is almost insurmountable. It is difficult because we all are almost inseparably interwoven with the 3D world, whether we want to admit it or not. And because, like with the Stockholm Syndrome, we feel so connected to our tormentors and to the more pleasant aspects that are available to us in their prison model, we cannot bring ourselves to leave them behind in the transition to 5D. This is one of the reasons why this transition has not happened yet. To emphasize it once again – our world functions due to the fact that deception, lies, misleading, and concealment are possible, and that these can be sold to us as something completely different, namely as a supposed truth. Thus, it is possible to separate us from the truth of our being. And this will be no longer possible in 5D. It is also no longer needed to work because whatever is needed can be materialized out of the quantum field. But how desirable will a luxury automobile be if everybody can obtain as many of them as they like at any time? Living in our 3D world includes that we live mostly in scarcity. There is always something that we think we still need, because we try to fill the hole in us which has arisen because we are not in touch with our very own life force. And all this happens while in the background we are faced every day with the fact that the coverage of our basic needs such as food, heating, water, clothing *etc.*, is by no means guaranteed. In order to be able to satisfy these basic needs, we must sell ourselves and struggle.

The motivation for our 3D world arises from the fact that people are forced to provide for themselves in the material world. This motivates those who are egomaniacal enough to keep these processes going for the earth-dominating powers, namely the politicians, bankers, big industrialists, IT architects, the disease system, the media, *etc.*

After all that has been discussed above, we may become aware that with the transition to 5D, the familiar 3D model automatically disintegrates from one moment to the next, because nothing of it makes sense anymore. And for one moment, also our entire life path in this incarnation and our entire value model no longer make sense. Letting go of all that is our greatest challenge, because the path up to this point has already cost us so much. If we are to let go (supposedly) of everything we have achieved at high cost, then this is an almost super-humanly large obstacle.

This letting go should not be so difficult for the voluntarily incarnated star-children, however, it seems to me that we are more strongly interwoven in the 3D earth-field than this has been foreseen, on the one hand through the genetic memories which have been passed on to us through our physical bodies, and on the other hand through the "radio interference" which we experience upon trying to connect to our Higher Self.

We now need a breakthrough that clearly connects us with the remembrance of our life's mission, with no room for speculations.

Since you have read this book up to this point, we can be quite sure that it has come to you to remind you that now it is urgent to awaken and to step into your power. That is why I ask you to connect with the others from our group, first through getting in touch with me and with the groups that we will then be able to build and then in a psychic way. You and the other readers carry the ingredients and the power to open the doors to the 5th dimension now.

Above we talked about what keeps people from opening to the 5th dimensional space. And in order to help them and to stand by their side, we are incarnated on earth at this time. We are allowed to leave behind pretty much everything that we have gained and fought for in this 3D world. However, we remain here for the transition of this earth plane into the 5th dimension. Above all, so that we, as people among people, stand by humanity and let the transition to 5D become the greatest joy and the greatest happiness that a human being has ever experienced.

How will we recognize someone who has realized 5D in their earthly embodiment?

We do so by the fact that this person radiates abundance and wholeness with every cell of their being. Someone who stays when we come to them with our infinite neediness. Someone who can give us freely of their abundance without depleting even a tiny bit of their own energy. And we do not need to worry even for a moment about how to make up for what we have just received.

What we and every other human being will receive in the process is the feeling of being at home and being loved unconditionally, we will feel how infinitely valuable we are and that we do not need to do anything at all for this feeling because this is our unchanging primordial state of being.

Just as someone who has lived for 10 years in complete darkness cannot be exposed to the light immediately and unfiltered, it is also not possible to step out of 3D into 5D just like that. For this to happen harmonically and in a measured way, you, and I, and all the other star children have come here onto earth. We are the ones who will lead the people and the levels of life of this earth into the light, in the respectful and loving way they deserve.

And because we will already be in the light when we begin with this, we do not need to charge anyone for it because we have already left this system and live in abundance. So, we can give and share unlimited abundance with absolutely everyone.

I also imagine it in such a way that after their awakening, each human being is aware at any time that they can stay in this new 5th dimensional earthly plane for as long as they want, that they can make peace with this level of experience, either in community or by themselves, and that there will be always someone who can help in any desired way for as long as it is needed.

Will there be people who will refuse the higher vibrational energies even in the company of the star children? That I cannot say, we will have to wait and see. One must open oneself to the light from the inside, and if this does not happen, then the physical and any other form of embodiment on earth will probably no longer be possible. The path which the earth community presently follows in 3D, will not come to a good end for anybody. And whichever way one wants to go about it, in the universe there is no place anymore for such a lowly vibrating level of being like the one in which we live just now.

It can therefore only go up from here. To make our very best and most loving contribution to this, would that not be a wonderful common goal for us?

Are you with us?

EPILOGUE

AWAKENING

In these times, we are in a war over our divine spark of light. Why, and for what reason, we will only be able to understand with our awakening. Our present vision is obscured by physical, spiritual, and mental manipulations. That is why there are so many discussions about almost all aspects of our being. This happens also to a great extent in the esoteric-spiritual community, although community is not necessarily the correct word here, because this area is rather characterized by many different and often contradictory views. There are many gifted spirits who are flooding us with theoretical knowledge and who reach and inspire many people, but who change next to nothing in the status quo. While we indulge in hopes for a glorious future or insights about our past, the global narrative continues to move forward undeterred.

It is important that we all focus on the essentials and on our awakening and our ascent to the 5th dimensional level of being. We must understand that all the global issues and the complex aspects hidden behind them only serve the purpose of keeping us away from exactly this step, and to lead us, ready for harvesting so to speak, into the grand finale of the separation from our souls.

That is why it is so important to find our own truth in our own heart, to let the energy flow freely through our chakras, and to connect with the quantum field.

The daily "new" news only serves the purpose of keeping people stuck in their lower chakras and survival fears. By working with the meditations of Dr. Joe Dispenza and the information in his book *Becoming Supernatural*, we get the knowledge we need to tune into the endless space of the quantum field. If we put this in the foreground of our actions, if we manage to put together the same vision as described above in the center of our manifestation work, then we will very soon open the gates into the light and our awakening.

It is you who can bring this about. Not Q, not the military, not a government leader, not a guru. You carry this world-changing potential within you, and that is why so much effort is being made to keep you from this realization.

Instead of listening to hours of podcasts every day or reading posts in alternative media, we should repeatedly use this time to set out on the path into the quantum field with our shared vision.

You and I — all of us together — we achieve this! That is what we are here for, that is what we have prepared ourselves for, and that is what we will remind each other of every day. It will be our common potential for love with which we will walk the last steps on the way into the light. And together we will celebrate probably the most beautiful moment in the existence of the universe, together with earthbound humanity and with our light families.

Everyone is allowed to be present at this moment, they must only be open to the light beforehand. I am looking forward to walking this path together with you. And I am happy that we have now found each other again.

Stefan

How to Contact Me

Should you wish to contact me, please find me at my web site: *https://StefanBeckerAwakening.com*. You will be able to read my latest articles there as well as communicate with me directly.

Acknowledgments

The German version of *Awakening* (*Erwachen*) had been completed in late August of 2022. While this had felt like a great accomplishment back then, it still takes quite some more effort to have your book published and to become able to reach out to the ones, I have undertaken this journey for. Namely you, my reader.

First, I need to thank my wife for not only bearing with me throughout the process of writing *Awakening* but for working alongside me through the finished parts of the manuscript and for taking on many of the tasks that an editorial team would usually take over in support of the author. It is her who is responsible for the linguistic finishing touches. Any clumsy wording that still remains is attributable to me alone. She also pointed out factual inconsistencies and made sure that I reproduced the names of authors and book titles correctly. And as we were undertaking the translation of the German manuscript by ourselves, she has been instrumental in making the English version happen.

Together with her I went through the process of researching and contacting publishers in the US which finally led us to ARIS Books / Kallisti Publishing. And here my gratitude goes to Anthony Raymond Michalski, my editor. Anthony responded to my proposal the next day and offered to publish *Awakening* through his then upcoming imprint ARIS Books. Thank you, Anthony, for your encouragement and your inspiration and support. As well I am most grateful to everyone at ARIS Books who worked so diligently to make *Awakening* happen.

Still all the above would not have been possible had there not been a very good friend who so much believed in my book that she made the financial support available that was needed on my part to finance the release of *Awakening*. My deepest gratitude goes out to my friend.

As well I am most grateful to the feedback of the very few readers of *Erwachen*, who have been giving me some very uplifting and encouraging feedbacks. You have been instrumental in motivating me to carry on and to push through with my endeavor to have my book "truly" published. We have made it

EPILOGUE

together at last.

Further, I would like to thank all the people from my family and my circle of friends and former colleagues who have inspired me through my life so far and broadened my spirit. Also, those who have guided me out of the deepest emotional valleys and who have stood by me as friends in difficult times. There is a list of some very special people without whom I would not have made it to this day, and without whose help I would have already given up several times. Thank you for believing in me.

And I thank you, the reader of my book, for your trust and for engaging with the topics of this book. Thank you for setting out on the path to awakening, a path I would very much like to walk together with you and all other readers right up to the finish line. I am looking forward to it!

January 14, 2024

Bibliography

Brandis, Mark. *Der Spiegelplanet*. Wurdack Verlag, 2013.

Calleman, Carl Johan. *The Mayan Calendar and the Transformation of Consciousness*. Bear & Company, 2004.

Calleman, Carl Johan *The Nine Waves of Creation: Quantum Physics, Holographic Evolution, and the Destiny of Humanity*. Bear & Company, 2016.

Cannon, Dolores. *The Three Waves of Volunteers and the New Earth*. Ozark Mountain Publishing, 2011.

Christopher, John. *The Tripods Collection: The White Mountains; The City of Gold and Lead; The Pool of Fire; When the Tripods Came*, Aladdin (boxed set edition), 2014.

Currivan, Jude. *The 13th Step: A Global Journey in Search of Our Cosmic Destiny*. Hay House UK, 2009.

Dispenza, Dr. Joe *Becoming Supernatural: How Common People are Doing the Uncommon*. Hay House Inc., 2019.

Donaldson, Stephen R. *Lord Foul's Bane (The Chronicles of Thomas Covenant the Unbeliever, Book 1)*. HarperVoyager, 2019.

Evans-Wentz, W. Y. *Tibet's Great Yogi Milarepa: A Biography from the Tibetan*. Pilgrims Publishing, 2002.

Freeland, Elana. *Under an Ionized Sky: From Chemtrails to Space Fence Lockdown*. Feral House, 2018.

Freiherr von Liechtenstein, Peter. *Freiheit durch Wahrheit: Band 1 "Wahrheit"*. BoD – Books on Demand,, 2020.

Freiherr von Liechtenstein, Peter. *Freiheit durch Wahrheit: Band 2 „Freiheit"*. BoD – Books on Demand, 2020.

Gatto, John Taylor. *Weapons of Mass Instruction: A Schoolteacher's Journey Through the Dark World of Compulsory Schooling*. New Society Publishers, 2010.

Hancock, Graham; Bauval, Robert. *The Message of the Sphinx: A Quest for the Hidden Legacy of Mankind*. Crown, 1997.

Hand Clow, Barbara. *Awakening the Planetary Mind: Beyond the Trauma of the Past to a New Era of Creativity*. Bear & Company, 2011.

Hand Clow, Barbara. *The Mayan Code: Time Acceleration and Awakening the World Mind*; Bear & Company, 2007.

Helliwell, Tanis. *Summer with the Leprechauns: the authorized edition.* Tanis Helliwell Corporation, 2011.

Icke, David. *The Trap: What it is, how it works, and how we escape its illusions.* David Icke Books, 2022.

Kandoussi, Senya. *We are all Avatars: Remembering our cosmic origins and purpose.* independently published, 2021.

Kerner, Nigel. *Grey Aliens and the Harvesting of Souls: The Conspiracy to Genetically Tamper with Humanity.* Bear & Company, 2010.

Kerner, Nigel. *Grey Aliens and Artificial Intelligence: The Battle between Natural and Synthetic Beings for the Human Soul.* Bear & Company, 2022.

Kharitidi, Olga. *Das weiße Land der Seele.* Allegria Taschenbuch, 2017.

Koontz, Dean. Jane Hawk Novels 5-book set containing: *The Silent Corner, The Whispering Room, The Crooked Staircase, The Forbidden Door, The Night Window.* Generic, 2020.

Lash, John Lamb. *Not in His Image: Gnostic Vision, Sacred Ecology, and the Future of Belief, 15th anniversary edition.* Chelsea Green Publishing, 2021.

Malkowski, Edward F. *Ancient Egypt 39,000 BCE: The History, Technology, and Philosophy of Civilization X.* Bear & Company, 2010.

Marciniak, Barbara. *Path of Empowerment: New Pleiadian Wisdom for a World in Chaos.* New World Library, 2004.

Marrs, Jim. *The Rise of the Fourth Reich: The Secret Societies That Threaten to Take Over America.* William Morrow Paperbacks, 2009.

Megre, Vladimir. *The Space of Love (The Ringing Cedars, Book 3).* Ringing Cedars Press, 2008.

Megre, Vladimir. *Co-Creation (The Ringing Cedars, Book 4).* Ringing Cedars Press, 2008.

Pogacnik, Marko. *Earth Changes, Human Destiny.* Findhorn Press, 2001.

Pogacnik, Marko. *Nature Spirits & Elemental Beings: Working with the Intelligence in Nature; Findhorn Press, 2nd edition.* Findhorn Press, 2010.

Radha, Swami Sivananda. *The Divine Light Invocation*. Timeless Books, 2010.

Radha, Swami Sivananda. *Time to Be Holy: Reflecting on Daily Life*. Timeless Books, 1996.

Robbins, Dianne. *Messages from the Hollow Earth*. Trafford on Demand Pub, 2003.

Sigdell, Jan Erik. *Reign of the Anunnaki: The Alien Manipulation of Our Spiritual Destiny*. Bear & Company, 2018.

Solara. *11 : 11: Inside the Doorway*. Star Borne Unltd, 1992.

Tag, Karin. *Die Prophezeiungen des Kristallschädels Corazon de Luz, Gebundene Ausgabe*. AMRA Verlag, 2009.

Walsch, Neale Donald. *Conversations with God: An Uncommon Dialogue, Book 1*. Hampton Roads Publishing, 1995.

Zettel, Christa. *Die Seele der Erde*. Taschenbuch; Bastei Lübbe, 1997.

LET'S MAKE A BOOK — NOT CONTENT

Content. Aren't you sick of that word and how it's used to describe music, videos, and, yes, even books?

These words that so many callously call "content" are ideas . . . tales . . . visions . . . hopes . . . dreams . . .

These ephemeral wisps were grasped from the ether and wrestled and wrought onto a sterile page.

They were molded and refined into stories . . . poems . . . histories . . . declarations . . . insights . . .

That's why at ARIS Books we believe that an author's words — *your words* — are more than just content.

They're a book — *your book.*

It's our hope, much like yours, that your book will be a beacon of knowledge, creativity, and passion. Thus, we focus on publishing books that readers — *your readers* — will cherish, share, and return to, not just scroll past.

Our unique publishing program is designed to bring your book to life and into the hands of eager readers — from manuscript development to global distribution.

Submit your manuscript to ARIS Books today and let's transform your idea — *your words* — into a lasting legacy.

Let's make *a book* — not content.

WWW.**ARISBooks**.COM

Thank you for getting my book Awakening. *I hope my words create a spark inside you that will awaken a light that shines in the world. You are invited to join me on my website where you can explore more of my thoughts and findings. I look forward to seeing you there . . .*

www.StefanBeckerAwakening.com

Made in the USA
Columbia, SC
12 August 2024